HOUSING POLICY IN ACTION
The new financial regime
for council housing

Peter Malpass, Matthew Warburton,
Glen Bramley and Gavin Smart

S·A·U·S

First published in Great Britain in 1993 by

SAUS Publications
School for Advanced Urban Studies
Rodney Lodge
Grange Road
Clifton
Bristol BS8 4EA

Telephone (0272) 741117
Fax (0272) 737308

British Library Cataloguing in Publication Data
A catalogue record for this book is available from the British Library

SAUS Study 8

ISBN   1 873575 47 5
ISSN   0268-3725

The School for Advanced Urban Studies is a centre for research, post-graduate and continuing education, and consultancy at the University of Bristol.   The School's focus is the analysis, development and implementation of policy in the fields of employment, health and social care, housing, social management, and urban change and government. Its aim is to bridge the gaps between theory and practice, between different policy areas, and between academic disciplines. SAUS is committed to the wide dissemination of its findings and in addition to courses and seminars the School has established several publications series: **SAUS Studies, Occasional Papers, Working Papers, Studies in Decentralisation and Quasi-Markets, DRIC Reports and SAUS Guides and Reports**.

SAUS is working to counter discrimination on grounds of gender, race, disability, age and sexuality in all its activities.

Printed in Great Britain by J. W. Arrowsmith Ltd., Bristol BS3 2NT.

CONTENTS

ACKNOWLEDGEMENTS

The research reported here was supported by the Joseph Rowntree Foundation between April 1990 and July 1992. The authors gratefully acknowledge the value of the Foundation's assistance in the execution of the research and the production of the report.

The production of the report has relied upon the help and cooperation of a considerable number of people. We owe thanks to all the officers and elected members in the case study authorities for their patient explanation of how the new financial regime had affected them and how they had responded to it; and to officials within the Department of the Environment for providing a wealth of authoritative statistical evidence as well as helpful advice and comment on policy implementation in central government. Helpful comments were provided by an advisory panel consisting of Richard Bramley, John Hills, Professor Peter Kemp, Professor Alan Murie, David Sands, Graham Saunders, David Smith and chaired by Michael Sturge.

Thanks are also due to Sue Mackay of the Faculty of the Built Environment, University of the West of England, Bristol, and Alison Shaw and her colleagues of SAUS Publications, School for Advanced Urban Studies.

Any errors of fact or interpretation are of course the responsibility of the authors alone.

ABBREVIATIONS

ACG	Annual capital guideline
ADC	Association of District Councils
ALA	Association of Local Authorities
AMA	Association of Metropolitan Authorities
BCA	Basic credit approval
CIPFA	Chartered Institute of Public Finance and Accountancy
CWD	Council of Welsh Districts
DOE	Department of the Environment
DSO	Direct Services Organisation
DSS	Department of Social Security
GNI	Generalised needs index
HAT	Housing Action Trust
HIP	Housing investment programme
HRA	Housing revenue account
LBA	London Boroughs Association
LSVT	Large scale voluntary transfer
M&M	Maintenance and management
NFR	New financial regime
PESC	Public Expenditure Survey Committee
RCCO	Revenue contribution to capital outlay
RFC	Rate fund contribution
RPI	Retail price index
RTIA	Receipts taken into account
SCA	Supplementary credit approvals
SCG	Specified capital grants
WO	Welsh Office

SUMMARY

The Local Government and Housing Act 1989 introduced a new framework for the revenue side of local authority housing finance, and for local authority capital finance across all services. This research on the implementation and impact of the new system reveals that while local authorities have been severely restricted in certain ways they retain the capacity and willingness to diverge from central government policy. Key findings include:

- Actual rent levels have increased by 47%, overshooting government guidelines by 12%.

- Resources for the repair and maintenance of the council stock have fallen dramatically, despite attempts by authorities to maintain programmes at the expense of even higher rents.

- Among its various objectives for the new system the government placed highest priority on controlling capital expenditure, and was less concerned with expenditure on management and maintenance.

- The housing element of the housing subsidy received by local authorities has been phased out for the majority; but the rent rebate subsidy (housing benefit) has risen because of rent increases. Together with transitional factors, this has meant that actual subsidies have exceeded Treasury estimates.

- Local autonomy has been significantly curbed, but some local discretion still exists and is indeed necessary.

- The attempt to target management and maintenance expenditure on areas of greatest need has not so far been particularly successful.

The context of the new financial regime

The Local Government and Housing Act 1989 introduced new arrangements for both revenue and capital finance. This research concentrated on the revenue side, covering issues to do with rents, management and maintenance (M&M) and subsidy. The new financial regime (NFR) was introduced to replace a system which had been in operation since 1981, and which had ceased to give central government the control that it desired over local policy and practice. The NFR was an attempt by the centre to restore a greater degree of control while leaving local authorities a certain amount of discretion. Despite the significance of the changes introduced in the 1989 Act and the adoption of a confusing new vocabulary of terms, the NFR represented considerable continuity with the old system. The key element of continuity was the retention of the payment of subsidy on the basis of notional changes in income and expenditure. Local authorities remain free to determine actual rents and spending, knowing that each pound of extra spending puts a pound on rents.

The NFR has to be understood in the context of government policy towards public expenditure as a whole. Housing policy objectives are constrained by this wider context, and priority has been given to limiting the aggregate subsidy bill. As well as giving authorities guidance on assumed increases in rents and M&M spending, the NFR is a mechanism for the annual distribution of an amount of subsidy which is set in advance in the government's public expenditure planning process. The leverage exerted on rents is produced not by the size of the guideline rent increase but by the difference between that guideline and the M&M allowance: the bigger the difference the greater the leverage. Thus a high guideline rent increase with a matching increase in M&M allowance produces less direct pressure on rents than a lower guideline increase paired with a nil increase in M&M allowance.

Policy objectives

In introducing the NFR, the government was explicitly committed to raising rents generally and to increasing rent differentials between authorities with high and low value stock. The government's objective in relation to M&M spending was less clearly stated, but there were suggestions that some authorities at least should be encouraged to spend more in order to provide a better service to tenants. The 1989 Act laid down the basic framework of the NFR but its impact on local authorities has been dependent on the annual subsidy determinations issued by the Department of the Environment (DOE) and Welsh Office (WO), and, in particular, on the rent guidelines and M&M allowances contained in those determinations.

Rents

On average the government has assumed that rents will rise by more than inflation each year since the start of the NFR; the average guideline rent has increased by 30% in three years. However, the policy of differential rent increases has meant that the impact has been very different from place to place. An authority in an area with low property values, charging the national average rent in 1989/90 and receiving the minimum guideline rent increase each year since 1990, would have been expected to increase its rents by 17%. However, an authority in a high value area, starting from the same rent and receiving the maximum guideline each year, would have faced a notional increase of 55% in three years.

In practice rents have risen sharply in real terms since the start of the NFR in April 1990 and by significantly more than the guideline increases, as the table below reveals. In 1992/93 the average council rent in England was 47% above the average for 1989/90 and 12% above the overall guideline. Some individual authorities have made increases of more than 100% since the start of the NFR.

Table A1: Actual and guideline rents 1989/90 to 1992/93 (England)

	1989/90	1990/91	1991/92	1992/93
DOE guideline rent (£ pw)	20.97	23.05	24.89	27.33
Average actual rent (£ pw)	20.70	23.76	27.25	30.55
Average rent as % of earnings	7.6%	7.9%	8.4%	8.9%

Source: DOE

Average rents are now above guideline in all regions and types of area. The margin is greatest in London and least in the North and in declining industrial areas, but the general tendency to exceed guidelines is apparent everywhere. This is in clear contrast to the trend during the 1980s. Authorities have shown marked variation in their rent increases, reflecting both the differential impact of the system in different areas and differences in local political responses.

Management and maintenance

Most of the divergence of actual rents from guidelines is explained by expenditure on management and maintenance in excess of the allowances. DOE figures suggest that average local authority budgeted spending on M&M in England in 1992/93 was 15.3% above the national average allowance. The other major contributory factor was the tendency for authorities to finance an increasing amount of capital outlay from rent income.

Expenditure on housing management has risen in real terms, continuing a trend established before the introduction of the NFR. Expenditure on repairs funded from rent income has also risen, but one of the most important findings to emerge from the research is that total expenditure on repair and maintenance has fallen in all areas, particularly in London and other cities where problems of disrepair tend to be worse. This fall is due to the new capital control system and the much-reduced availability of capital receipts. The fall has been offset to only a small extent by higher spending financed directly from rents. Since 1991/92 the government has operated a system of targeting M&M allowances to encourage low spending authorities, but the evidence clearly shows that the loss of access to capital receipts has resulted in a less well targeted pattern of expenditure on the local authority stock in England. This is particularly worrying in view of the much-discussed backlog of repairs in the public sector housing stock.

Subsidy

The housing revenue account subsidy (HRA) consists of two parts, the housing element (which may be negative) and the rent rebate element. The NFR gave government the power to reduce the rent rebate subsidy by the amount of any negative entitlement to the housing element; in a majority of English local authorities the housing element of the HRA is now a negative amount. However, because authorities have generally raised rents by more than guideline amounts they have increased their expenditure on rent rebates. This, together with other transitional effects, resulted in actual subsidy expenditure exceeding the budgeted amounts by over £500 million in 1990/91 and £200 million in 1991/92. Overruns of this kind have an effect on both relations between the DOE and the Treasury, and on the way that the Treasury approaches budget setting in subsequent years. Under the 1980 Housing Act subsidy system, authorities started to go out of subsidy in large numbers after the first two years, but this is not happening on the same scale in the NFR. Fewer than 20 authorities have lost all subsidy entitlement, and the majority of these are authorities which have transferred all their stock to new landlords. In this sense the NFR is proving to be more robust than its predecessor.

Central-local relations

Local authorities have suffered a significant loss of autonomy since the introduction of the NFR; the ring-fence around the HRA means that they can no longer draw on their local tax income to support the housing service, nor can they transfer HRA surpluses into their general funds. However, the main way in which loss of control is experienced by most authorities is in terms of the loss of access to their accumulated capital receipts. The HRA ring-fence has presented fewer problems to local authorities than had been expected, partly because it has not been fully implemented. The research found that authorities were generally more concerned about the effects of the capital control system and the much reduced level of resources for investment in improving their housing stocks.

Experience with the NFR shows that local authorities are not very easy to 'steer', except in the aggregate, especially where there is only one hard policy instrument, namely the amount of subsidy. The evidence suggests that local authorities have retained sufficient freedom to produce a wide range of responses to the impact of the NFR. Nevertheless, where authorities are given less subsidy they tend to increase rents to maintain or increase expenditure on M&M, and where they receive more subsidy they generally respond by raising M&M expenditure.

The evidence suggests that ministers have given greater weight to the aim of keeping rents on the move in real terms than raising expenditure on management and maintenance. In effect they have preferred to take criticism for under-estimating the need to increase M&M spending rather than for large increases in rents.

About the research

The research was carried out over the first two and a quarter years of the NFR. It involved two distinct strands of work: an analysis of statistical data for all local authorities in England, and two rounds of 15 case studies covering a range of authorities of different types and sizes in different parts of England and Wales. The case studies were an essential complement to the analysis of national data and were designed to get at the processes through which local authorities arrived at their responses to the NFR. The national statistics for all authorities were provided by DOE, the Chartered Institute of Public Finance and Accountancy (CIPFA) and the Association of District Councils (ADC)/Association of Metropolitan Authorities (AMA) survey.

Update, December 1992

This research project was completed in July 1992, and the text of the report concentrates on explaining and interpreting the development of the NFR up to that point. However, it is appropriate to refer briefly to subsequent developments. First, in his autumn statement the chancellor announced that for a limited period, November 1992 to December 1993, local authorities would be able to spend 100% of new capital receipts. This must be seen as welcome, but it does nothing to release accumulated receipts, and the impact of this temporary concession is unlikely to be substantial given the current low level of council house sales and the offsetting reductions elsewhere in the capital programme.

Second, on the revenue side, the determination of rent guidelines and M&M allowances for 1993/94 appears to continue the trends established in previous years, although the squeeze on M&M spending is tighter. The guideline rent increases for 1993/94 range from £1.50 to £3.00 per week. Over one third (126) of English authorities have the maximum guideline increase. These authorities are heavily concentrated in the eastern region, London, and the south east and south west of the country. Maximum guideline increases are very rare in other regions.

The M&M allowances for 1993/94 are based on an overall increase of 1% in real terms, but 57% of English authorities have their allowances frozen at 1992/93 levels. Moreover, more than a fifth of authorities have a nil M&M increase coupled with a maximum £3.00 per week guideline rent increase. In the coming year authorities which receive any increase at all in M&M allowance - even as low as £1.00 per dwelling per year - are defined by the DOE as beneficiaries of targeting. This may be seen as a development which, if continued, will bring the whole notion of targeting into disrepute.

INTRODUCTION

In April 1990 the government introduced a new financial regime (NFR) for local authority housing in England and Wales, replacing a subsidy system which had been in place since 1981. At the same time it also introduced a new framework for controlling local authority capital expenditure across all services. Together these two new systems made major changes to the environment of controls and accounting conventions in which local authority housing finance operates. At the start of the 1980s the systems then put in place were seen to give the government considerably increased control over local authority policy decisions, but within a short period both the subsidy system and the capital control system began to break down as local authorities broke free from the constraints. The Local Government and Housing Act 1989 represented a renewed attempt by the government to reassert its control of local authority housing finance and local authority capital finance as a whole.

In addition to its impact on councils and their tenants, the NFR is, therefore, of interest in terms of central-local government relations and the dynamics of policy implementation. It is also important to locate the NFR in relation to debates about the reform of housing finance, and to place it in the context of the wider restructuring of housing policy in the late 1980s. This opening chapter seeks to contextualise the NFR and the research which is discussed in subsequent chapters.

The reform of housing finance

The reform of housing finance in Britain has been much discussed over the last 20 years, since the issue was brought to the fore in the early 1970s by two main factors. First, the highly contentious Housing Finance Act 1972 introduced a radical recasting of pricing and subsidy systems for rented housing, and second, the rapid rise in house prices in 1972/73 drew public attention to the economics of the housing market, and in particular to the escalating cost of financial assistance to mortgaged home owners through tax relief. In 1974 the government announced the establishment of a fundamental review of housing finance, across all tenures, with the objective of securing a more equitable and balanced distribution of assistance amongst tenants and home owners. However, the results of the review were not published until 1977 (Department of the Environment and Welsh Office, 1977), by which time the political climate had changed significantly, and government commitment to fundamental cross-tenure reform had disappeared (Lansley, 1979; Merrett, 1979). The main policy measures to emerge from the 1977 Green Paper were the Housing Investment Programme (HIP) system for planning and regulating local authority capital expenditure, and the principles of a new local authority housing subsidy system.

In the mid 1980s, the debate on housing finance reform was given renewed impetus by the report of the inquiry into British housing, chaired by the Duke of Edinburgh (National Federation of Housing Associations, 1985). The thrust of the report's proposals was that reform should be seen as a package affecting all tenures and aimed at producing a more equitable and efficient housing system. Underlying these proposals, and those of most of the other contributions to the debate, is the notion of tenure neutrality, or a level playing field on which investors, producers and consumers could make choices unfettered by financial advantages and disadvantages in different tenures (Hills, 1991, Chapter 16). The inquiry report's proposals for fundamental reform were instantly dismissed by government ministers, but the debate continued. A major programme of housing finance research was commissioned by the Joseph Rowntree Foundation (Maclennan, Gibb and More, 1991), and the inquiry team was subsequently reassembled to produce a second report (Joseph Rowntree Foundation, 1991). Again the government displayed a complete lack of interest in fundamental cross-tenure reform which would involve action on mortgage interest relief as well as subsidies in rented housing. Meanwhile, however, the government had introduced the new financial regime for local authority housing in 1990.

The purpose of this brief historical summary of attempts to stimulate policy action to reform housing finance is to highlight the point that although successive governments, both Conservative and Labour, have turned their faces against fundamental cross-tenure measures they have been far from inactive in reforming housing finance. Whilst rejecting calls for the replacement of mortgage interest relief and the creation of a level playing field in housing finance, governments have pressed ahead with their own reform agendas concentrating on the rented sectors. A key factor in the housing policy agenda of governments since 1979 has been that a commitment to the expansion of individual home ownership has been given consistently higher priority than objectives about equity and efficiency in housing finance. Indeed, the commitment to tenure restructuring has produced a tolerance of huge distortions in the housing market and the acceptance of massive, and highly inequitably distributed, support for mortgaged home owners.

The restructuring of housing policy

Market-based housing systems are dynamic and constantly changing in response to both developments in the wider economy and policy interventions by governments, although the capacity of policy makers to influence the underlying nature and direction of change should not be over-estimated. However, when one political party is in power for a prolonged period it has the opportunity to stamp its ideological footprint firmly on the course of policy development, and in Britain since 1979 the Conservative Party has energetically pursued a particular vision of housing provision (Malpass and Murie, 1990, Chapter 5; Malpass, 1993). In the early 1980s, British housing policy was directed towards the expansion of home ownership, mainly through the sale of council houses, and little attention was paid to the production of policies to meet the continuing need for rented housing.

The year 1980 marked a turning point in the development of council housing; until then the number of council houses had grown steadily every year for sixty years, and every year since then the number has declined. The sale of a million and a half council dwellings by 1990 (Forrest and Murie, 1992, p 139) produced a huge flow of capital receipts, and nearly matched the receipts from all other privatisations put together in the period 1979/80 to 1989/90 (Joseph Rowntree Foundation, 1991, p 71). At the same time the rate of new building was falling to the lowest peacetime levels since the early 1920s. These developments not only severely affected the supply of rented housing but also transformed the finances of local housing authorities and brought new issues onto the policy agenda.

Despite the success of the right to buy legislation, the rate of sales fell after the peak of 1982 and the government began to look for further ways to reduce the size of the public sector stock, while at the same time acknowledging the continuing need for rented housing. From the early part of 1987 it became clear that the government was beginning to turn its attention to rented housing and to recognise that a policy concentrating overwhelmingly on increasing home ownership was inadequate (Platt, 1987). Ministers presided over what the current housing minister has described as a "fundamental and much needed review" of housing policy (Young, 1991, p 8) culminating in a series of announcements in the run-up to the general election of May 1987 and the subsequent production of a White Paper (Department of the Environment and Welsh Office, 1987) setting out proposals affecting the rented sectors. Having come into office in the late 1970s with a clear and well worked out, if narrow, housing policy, the Conservatives approached the end of the 1980s with a need to devise new measures; partly to broaden the base of housing policy, partly to maintain the momentum of existing policies and partly to respond to problems arising from the implementation of earlier legislation.

The new proposals did not imply any weakening of the government's enthusiasm for home ownership; they broadened and strengthened housing policy by adding a strategy designed to promote the provision of rented housing. The package of proposals confirmed the government's commitment to deregulation and privatisation, and its willingness to take a very interventionist stance in relation to local authorities. The approach was based on three main elements:

● a revival of investment in private rented housing, stimulated by deregulation of rents, and later supported by tax breaks through the business expansion scheme;

● expansion of housing association provision on the basis of lower grant rates, increased use of private finance and a phasing out of the system of regulated tenancies and fair rents;

- a reduced role for local authorities as providers of rented housing, but an enhanced role as enablers of other providers: housing associations and private landlords.

The strategy was carried forward in the Housing Act 1988 which deregulated new lettings in the private rented sector from January 1989 (Crook et al, 1991; Kemp, 1988; 1993), and brought in a new financial regime for housing associations (Randolph, 1993). It also introduced radical provisions for the transfer of local authority housing to new owners. The government's hostility to local authorities as owners and managers of rented housing was such that it believed a significant number of tenants who wished to continue renting would choose to transfer to new landlords. It also believed that the run-down nature of some council estates justified ministerial intervention compulsorily to transfer these estates to newly established Housing Action Trusts (HATs) (Woodward, 1991; Karn, 1993).

The deregulation of private renting, and the move to increased reliance on private finance and assured tenancies in the housing association sector, were essentially supply-side measures intended to make it easier for landlords and associations to expand production. Implicit in the strategy were substantially higher rent levels, albeit underpinned by housing benefit for low income households. Higher rents implied additional measures aimed at stimulating demand. Constraints on the supply, quality and price of local authority housing were, therefore, a logical next step and the NFR can be seen in this context.

Policy implementation

In an early contribution to the literature on implementation Pressman and Wildavsky asserted confidently that "a verb like 'implement' must have an object like 'policy'" (1973, p iv) but subsequent critics have pointed out that matters are generally rather more complicated, and this is certainly true in the case of the NFR. The Pressman and Wildavsky formulation represents a top-down view of the policy process, and implies that policy must precede implementation. It also implies a clear hierarchy in which policy is made at, or close to, the top and then implemented by those lower down. Writers using this perspective assume that it is possible to compare the initial policy with the outcomes and to measure any mismatch between intent and outcome in terms of a series of 'implementation deficits'. These deficits reflect the lack of complete harmony between actors at different stages in the policy process, the inference being that the larger the number of stages, the greater will be the risk of significant implementation deficit. This is almost a Chinese whispers view of implementation and leads to the conclusion that in order to secure its favoured outcomes the top should get a tighter grip on things at the bottom.

However, other writers have argued that a bottom-up approach produces a better explanation of the policy process (Elmore, 1980; Barrett and Fudge, 1981). This perspective recognises that the actors and agencies actually involved in implementation have objectives and preferences of their own and that their view of what constitutes successful implementation is likely to reflect local circumstances, rather than, or as well as, centrally defined criteria. Between these two approaches there is clearly the theoretical space to develop a third perspective which seeks in some way to combine the top and bottom in an interactive relationship.

In the context of the British system of government it is clear that central and local government are hierarchically related. Local authorities can be made and abolished by an Act of Parliament, as happened in 1986 when a whole tier of local government (in London and the largest English conurbations) was removed. But this does not necessarily imply a top-down approach to policy. The fact that local authorities are democratically elected bodies with their own revenue raising powers means that they are more than the agents of central government. The localities may depend to a large extent on financial resources provided or authorised by the centre, but the centre also depends on the authorities for the delivery of many key services. There is, therefore, a situation of mutual dependency, albeit one in which the balance of power is generally tilted towards the centre (Rhodes, 1981). The centre may set out a framework for policy but local authorities are policy-making bodies in their own right and retain some freedom to interpret central policy in the light of local circumstances and preferences.

This suggests that the implementation of policies such as the NFR should not be seen in simple terms implying that the centre makes policy and the local authorities implement it. And yet the NFR is clearly a top-down policy, conceived at the centre as a way of getting a tighter grip on things at the local level. If outcomes can be shown to depart from those intended by the centre, then what is the cause? Explanations would need to consider local level factors such as the circumstances varying from those predicted by the centre, or local actors failing to grasp or share central policy makers' objectives. Other factors might arise at the centre to the extent that policy makers fail to frame legislation in a way which ensures outcomes in line with objectives (Ingram and Schneider, 1990). A bottom-up perspective, on the other hand, suggests that policy outcomes might vary from central objectives because of the extent to which implementing bodies are also involved in policy-making activities of their own. As a result they receive central policy not as a set of instructions or guiding principles referring to shared objectives, but as a barrier or constraint on existing locally determined policy. In this context, implementation becomes a struggle between top and bottom, the outcome of which depends on the way the top has framed its legislation and the ingenuity and political determination of the bottom. An understanding of the policy/action relationship requires consideration of the interpretation and reformulation of central policy by local level institutions whose resourcefulness in terms of ignoring, avoiding or exploiting legislation should not be under-estimated.

It is also important to think of the implementation of the NFR as a process in which the centre is actively and continuously involved. This is not a policy area in which the centre provides a legislative framework and then stands back from the implementation process. The central departments in England and Wales are actively engaged in trying to steer local authorities towards outcomes preferred by the centre.

The research

The policy approach

Most work on housing finance (Hills, 1991; Garnett, Reid and Riley, 1991; Gibb and Munro, 1991; Maclennan, Gibb and More, 1991) falls within the boundaries of applied economics. The research reported here, however, adopts a different perspective which can be described as a policy approach. Much has been written about the level of rents which, in the view of those proposing reform, ought to be charged by local authorities, and about the appropriate level and form of subsidy. There has been much less, however, about how far, and by what means, local authorities can be persuaded or coerced to set rents at particular levels. A policy approach is concerned with issues of implementation as well as policy design; it is concerned with central-local government relations and with the politics of policy as well as the measurement of outcomes.

Aims of the research

This report is based on research undertaken since April 1990, looking at the implementation of the NFR with respect to the revenue side of housing finance; covering issues around rents, management and maintenance (M&M) expenditure and subsidy. The aims of the research were:

- to determine, as far as possible, the objectives underlying the introduction of the new regime, and to identify any difference between the objectives espoused by different central departments;

- to examine the implementation of the new regime at both the national and local level;

- to evaluate the extent to which the policy objectives are realised, and to identify any possible modification of objectives over time;

- to draw general conclusions about implementation processes and issues in relation to the reform of local authority housing finance.

Methodology

The research consisted of monitoring the implementation of the NFR during its first two years, with some discussion of plans for the third year. This involved analysis of aggregate data for each year and two rounds of case studies with local authorities in different circumstances and different parts of the country. The initial intention was to use the data on housing revenue accounts (estimates and actuals) published by the Chartered Institute of Public Finance and Accountancy (CIPFA). In the event, an approach was made to the Department of the Environment (DOE) who were able to provide access to their own more comprehensive and reliable statistics based on subsidy claim forms returned by

English local authorities for 1991/92. Some data was also obtained from the Association of Metropolitan Authorities (AMA) and Association of District Councils (ADC) 1992 housing finance survey which was processed by members of the research team in parallel with this study.

The local case studies were an essential part of the research and an important complement to the statistical analysis. They were designed to get behind the published outcome figures and to explore the factors which led to both particular outcomes and the decision-making processes involved. Two rounds of visits were carried out. Most of the authorities were visited in both 1990/91 and 1991/92, and in-depth interviews were conducted with a range of key actors, including senior officers and usually the chair of the Housing Committee.

Guide to the book

In this book, Chapter 1 looks at the reasons behind the introduction of the NFR; here and throughout the book the emphasis is clearly on the revenue side of local authority housing finance, although reference is made to the capital side and to the ways in which the two interact. In general, reference to the capital side is confined to areas of interaction with the revenue side. Chapter 2 outlines the basic principles and elements of the NFR, without attempting to describe every detail of the more exotic features of the system. Chapter 3 looks at the way it has been operated since 1990 and refers to the main outcomes in terms of national and regional analysis. It is in this chapter that reference is made to the implementation of the NFR by central government. Chapter 4 presents the results of the analysis of data on the impact of the NFR at regional and local level. In addition to looking at developments since 1990, the chapter uses data from 1987/88 to provide a somewhat longer-term perspective. Chapter 5 draws on the case studies to examine some of the issues lying behind the overall picture set out in Chapters 3 and 4, and the final chapter presents the conclusions. A glossary of terms is provided on p 104 in order to assist those readers unfamiliar with recent housing finance terms, as well as a full list of abbreviations used within the text on p viii.

The book is based on research on a complex and often very technical area of housing policy, but its objectives are to engage with a wider set of debates about central-local government relations and policy implementation as well as housing finance. The book is, and policy implementation as well as housing finance. The book is, therefore, written in a way which seeks to present the housing finance issues in language which is accessible to non-specialists in this arcane area of research.

one

WHY A 'NEW FINANCIAL REGIME'?

Introduction

The Local Government and Housing Act 1989 came exactly seventy years after the introduction of Exchequer subsidies for local authority housing. It was the nineteenth in a series of Acts in which successive governments have sought either to fine-tune or radically alter the subsidy system and, therefore, it has raised questions about why continued intervention of this kind has been seen to be necessary (Malpass, 1992). This chapter looks at the issues involved in local authority housing finance and its reform, concentrating on the revenue side but taking account of the importance of the capital side and the way that capital and revenue interconnect.

The distinction between capital and revenue is fundamental to an understanding of housing finance, and yet it is a distinction which is often rather arbitrary (Garnett, Reid and Riley, 1991, p 5; Gibb and Munro, 1991, p 68; Hepworth, 1984, pp 9-11). The conventional approach is to regard expenditure on durable items, such as houses, as capital expenditure, while expenditure on staffing and day-to-day running costs is placed in the revenue account. It is important to remember, however, that it is only the initial cost of durable items which counts as capital expenditure: whereas the regular repayment of debt and interest arising from borrowing for capital projects counts as revenue expenditure, since it is paid out of the flow of revenue income. In the case of public housing, revenue income is now mainly in the form of rents and subsidies, although until 1990 local authorities had the power to draw income from local taxes (the rates) and in the 1980s significant revenue income was generated from interest earned on invested receipts arising from the sale of capital assets.

The main ways that the capital and revenue accounts interact are:

● when borrowing to finance capital expenditure gives rise to loan charges which have to be met from revenue income;

● when capital expenditure is met directly from revenue income;

● when items (such as small scale repairs), which are normally charged to revenue, are capitalised and funded by borrowing or by use of capital reserves;

● when invested capital reserves give rise to interest which counts as revenue income; if such reserves are then disposed of (eg for new building) there would be an impact on the revenue account in the form of reduced income from interest, but if the reserves were used to repay debt the impact would involve a compensating reduction in debt charges.

This report refers to the capital side primarily insofar as it interacts with the revenue-side issues of rents and subsidies.

Rents and subsidies

Throughout much of the period when local authorities were encouraged to build new houses, the financial issues were concerned with access to loan finance and the need for revenue subsidies. High levels of new building were associated with high debt ratios and revenue deficits. For many years the standard approach to subsidy was to provide £x for y years for each house. Towards the end of the 1960s, however, systems based on fixed annual payments per dwelling came to be seen as unsuitable in an inflationary environment and in an era of declining investment in new building. Over the last twenty years, successive British governments have sought an effective, politically acceptable and durable method of subsidising local authority housing. In terms of pricing and subsidy, the problem has been how to create a system which requires rents to rise in line with prices, and which provides subsidy for any deficit on the housing revenue account (HRA) after allowing for reasonable expenditure on items such as management and maintenance and debt charges. In governmental terms the problem is the tension between, on the one hand, the Treasury's need to manage public expenditure, and in particular to limit its own liability for subsidy, and on the other hand, the aspirations of local authorities to make and implement their own housing policies. If the Treasury is to underwrite HRA deficits then the key issues are about who decides local income and expenditure: who is to set the rents and who is to say what is an appropriate level of management and maintenance expenditure?

The Housing Finance Act 1972 was the first legislative attempt to grapple with this problem, establishing a principled approach to rent setting in the sense that rents were to be fixed according to the same criteria as private sector 'fair rents', and outside the control of local councils. However, the Act failed on political and technical grounds and was repealed in 1975 (Malpass, 1990, pp 114-35). The Housing Act 1980 represented a new approach to the same basic set of issues. This time the problem was implicitly formulated in terms of the desire to obtain control of the volume of subsidy, without completely eroding local autonomy. Whereas the 1972 Act had placed the emphasis on a principled approach to rent setting, the 1980 system contained no such principles, and instead the emphasis was placed on giving the centre the power to reduce subsidy. This was achieved by an important breakthrough in the form of the notional HRA which became the basis for the calculation of subsidy irrespective of the state of the actual HRA. The use of the notional HRA permitted a return to financial leverage as the means of exerting central government pressure on local rents. The advantage of this approach was that it preserved both limits to central government's financial liability and an element of local autonomy.

Under the 1980 Act system, subsidy was paid according to central government assumptions of year-on-year changes in income and expenditure; in practice standard assumptions were applied across the country, although the secretary of state had the power to make differential determinations. Local authorities remained free to set their own rents and expenditure on management and maintenance. They were also free to draw on the rates to supplement rent income, and were permitted to budget for HRA surpluses which could be transferred to support rate fund expenditure. In terms of central-local relations, the adoption of a notional HRA gave the centre considerable power whilst providing local authorities with no opportunity for public defiance of the exercise of that power. It was, therefore, a highly potent and successful device for reducing subsidy and raising rents: in the first year of operation, 1981/82, council rents rose by 48% on average, and in three years the real value of general subsidy fell by over 80% (Malpass, 1990, p 141).

However, the 1980 Act system soon began to lose its potency because leverage on rents was dependent upon there being some subsidy to withdraw. It very quickly became clear that a majority of authorities were going 'out of subsidy'. The government in the early 1980s lacked the political will to utilise other powers which it possessed to put further financial pressure on rents by reducing the rate support grant of those authorities whose notional HRAs were in surplus. In the face of opposition from Conservative-controlled councils, the government gave way and conceded: first, that a majority of councils would be released from direct central government pressure to raise rents; and second, where authorities chose to raise rents to levels which produced HRA surpluses, then those surpluses would be available to enhance local expenditure on non-housing services with no reduction in rate support grant. This concession was good for local authorities but it fatally undermined the coherence of the revenue side of council housing finance, which meant that eventually the government would move to reform it.

By the mid 1980s it was becoming clear that, from the government's point of view, the revenue side of council housing finance contained a number of undesirable features mainly associated with the volume, distribution and control of subsidy, and the complexity of the system. There were three sources of subsidy to HRAs:

● general housing subsidy, paid under the Housing Act 1980, where there was a notional deficit on the HRA;

● rate fund contributions (RFCs), which were determined by local authorities, but which were in some cases supported by central government through the rate support grant although the level of support was based on notional rather than actual contributions;

● rent rebate subsidy, which met 97.5% of the aggregate entitlement to housing benefit amongst authorities' tenants.

Central government had control of only one of these forms of financial assistance to council housing - general housing subsidy - and in practice its control was limited, so that some authorities received subsidy even though their actual HRAs were in surplus. It also emerged that RFCs were not generally closely related to the levels assumed by the DOE for rate support grant purposes. All authorities received substantial amounts of rent rebate subsidy irrespective of 'need' for subsidy in terms of the overall relationship between income and expenditure within the HRA. Thus there were issues about the distribution and use of subsidy involving questions of equity between tenants, rate payers and tax payers. There were also issues about efficiency and effectiveness in housing management to the extent that subsidies could distort the relationship between rents paid and quality of service received. By the late 1980s the government was convinced that further legislation was required, and a consultation paper was issued setting out proposals for a new financial regime for the revenue side of local authority housing (Department of the Environment, 1988).

The problem for the government was that it saw the level of overall Exchequer support for local authority HRAs as too high, in the sense that many authorities receiving substantial amounts of housing subsidy and/or rent rebate subsidy actually had large HRA surpluses which they transferred into their general rates funds. At the same time, the government perceived council rents generally to be too low, especially in relation to what people in the private sector paid for their housing. One particular buttress of low rents was the freedom to make rate fund contributions, and the White Paper of 1987 referred to "indiscriminate subsidies from the rates to hold down rents" as a "waste of resources" (Department of the Environment and Welsh Office, 1987, p 2), indicating an intention to remove this area of local autonomy. The government also drew on arguments (eg Audit Commission, 1986a, p 9; Power, 1987, p 8) which led it to the conclusion that "short term political factors can override efficient and economic management of housing in the long term, leading to unrealistically low rents and wholly inadequate standards of maintenance" (Department of the Environment and Welsh Office, 1987, p 3).

However, the 1980 Act subsidy system tended to prioritise rent increases over increases in management and maintenance. In most years the ministerial determinations of changes in M&M spending were based on the assumption that expenditure should be increased in line with an appropriate rate of inflation, implying that the underlying 'need to spend' on management and maintenance was broadly constant. Thus while the government criticised authorities for low spending on repairs, the subsidy system contained little incentive for them to spend more.

There are a number of reasons to question this assumption.

(i)   Since the mid 1980s, many authorities have made strenuous efforts to improve their repairs service: improving response times, quality of work and the number of repairs carried out. While it can be argued that the implied additional costs are offset by savings from increasing the proportion of programmed repairs (Audit Commission, 1986b), and from the spread of competitive tendering, there is no reason to suppose that increased costs and savings should have precisely cancelled each other out.

(ii) The average age of the housing stock is increasing, implying an increasing maintenance need.

(iii) During the second half of the 1980s, many authorities capitalised an increasing proportion of their repairs, partly because of the availability of capital receipts and the fact that capitalised repairs could be financed from the 'non-prescribed' part of these receipts. The NFR for capital affected this practice by reducing the usable part of receipts to 25%, and stipulating that repairs could only be capitalised if they 'enhanced' dwellings. During 1989 there was considerable debate between the DOE and the local authority associations about the implications of these changes. The AMA, the London Boroughs Association (LBA) and the Association of Local Authorities (ALA) argued that around £300 million in capitalised repairs would have to be transferred to the revenue account as a result of the new capital rules to maintain the same level of service. This would have implied a real increase in the national aggregate allowance of around 15% between 1989/90 and 1990/91, compared with the 3% real increase that was allowed in partial recognition of this argument.

(iv) On the management side, there have been widespread efforts to improve housing management, particularly through de-centralisation and customer care initiatives. The Audit Commission (1986a) had already noted that housing management expenditure was rising faster than inflation in the first half of the 1980s. It can be argued that the increased costs of decentralisation may be offset by increased income from fewer empty dwellings and better rent arrears recovery, but this will appear on the other side of the HRA.

(v) It is arguable that the increasing proportion of low income tenants and the widening gap between benefit levels and average earnings is tending to increase the degree of difficulty of the management task and hence the cost of delivering a standard level of service.

(vi) As the stock declines through right to buy and other sales, unit costs may tend to rise due to the presence of fixed costs and economies of scale.

Issues on the capital side

Formal controls on housing capital spending had only been introduced in the 1970s, and during the 1980s central government sought to control local authority expenditure via a system of capital allocations (which set limits on borrowing) and regulations covering the use of capital receipts. When the right to buy was introduced in 1980, the government allowed English authorities to augment their HIP allocations by up to 50% (the 'prescribed proportion') of capital receipts from the sale of dwellings (Welsh authorities could spend up to 100% of receipts). For English authorities the prescribed proportion was reduced to 40% in 1984 and then to 20% in 1985.

There were four particular aspects of the way the system worked in relation to housing which led the government to seek further change in the law. First, the pattern of council house sales after 1980 was geographically uneven (Forrest and Murie, 1988) leading to the accumulation of very substantial capital receipts in some areas while other areas had many fewer. It was often the case that the authorities with substantial receipts had less need or inclination to spend on housing investment than those authorities with fewer receipts. Part of the explanation for the reductions in the proportion of receipts which could be re-invested lies in the government's wish to effect a redistribution of spending power from receipt-rich authorities to receipt-poor authorities through the HIP system within given public expenditure planning levels.

Second, it became clear after the passage of the Local Government, Planning and Land Act 1980 that authorities had the power to spend not only the prescribed proportion of each year's capital receipts but also the same share of the remainder (the non-prescribed proportion) from previous years.   Thus receipts were said to cascade from one year to another allowing authorities to spend much more than had been anticipated.

Third, authorities had the power to spend the non-prescribed proportion on the renovation of their own stock.   This later became associated with the capitalisation of repairs expenditure, which not only allowed authorities to dispose of receipts in a way which improved the quality of the stock but in some cases led to the use of receipts instead of revenue income.   In other words, capitalisation of repairs could be a way of keeping rent increases to a minimum. The effect of capitalised repairs was that the recorded level of repairs expenditure within the HRA understated the true level of expenditure on the stock, and this later had the effect of depressing the baseline M&M allowance.

Fourth, interest on unspent receipts was credited to the HRA and, therefore, constituted a source of income which could be used at the discretion of the authority; some used the money to fund transfers to the general fund, while others used it as a means of keeping rents down or to raise M&M spending.

During the 1980s, capital and revenue side issues came together to produce a situation in which the government wished to make major changes.   The policies of higher rents, lower rates on new building, and promotion of council house sales transformed the financial circumstances of many local authorities creating new policy problems.   For the first time HRA surpluses and capital receipts came onto the policy agenda.   The initial legislative attempts to deal with these issues foundered in the face of local authority resistance, in the case of HRA surpluses, and local authority ingenuity in the exploitation of loopholes in the law in the case of capital receipts.   Another source of income used by authorities to support income from rents was interest on accumulated capital receipts; and the more the government discouraged authorities from re-investing receipts the more income they generated.   Thus the government needed to find a way (i) to reduce the total amount of Exchequer assistance flowing into local authority HRAs, (ii) to stop councils using RFCs to counter subsidy system leverage on rents, and (iii) to stop authorities from using capital receipts as a source of income to hold down rents.   These three requirements gave rise to key features of the NFR which are discussed in the next chapter.

two

THE NEW FINANCIAL REGIME

This chapter sets out a brief account of the new financial regime introduced in the Local Government and Housing Act 1989. Part IV of the Act introduced a new system for the control of local authority borrowing and capital expenditure on all services, and Part VI set out the provisions governing the revenue side of local authority housing.

The new housing revenue regime

In the consultation paper the government set three objectives for the new system (Department of the Environment, 1988, pp 5-6):

(i) It should be simpler, so that subsidy works in a more intelligible way and gives consistent incentives.

(ii) It should be fairer towards tenants and charge payers alike, and fairer between tenants in different areas. Rents generally should not exceed levels within the reach of people in low paid employment, and in practice they will frequently be below market levels. They should, however, be set by reference to these two parameters: what people can pay, and what the property is worth, rather than by reference to historic cost accounting figures.

(iii) It should be more effective, directing the available subsidy to those areas where it is needed, and providing an incentive for good management rather than a cover for bad practice and inefficiency.

The first of these objectives is uncontroversial, although more easily stated than achieved. The second is by no means new; it has been a continuing theme of government policy since the late 1960s that councils should be persuaded to charge rents closer to market levels while remaining in some sense affordable. The aim is both to reap the claimed efficiency advantages of market pricing, and assist the revival of the private rented sector, while at the same time economising on Exchequer support in the form of subsidy. The third objective refers to the reconstitution of the HRA as a 'landlord account', separated, or ring-fenced, from the other accounts of the local authority, and establishing a closer relationship between the rents paid by tenants and the cost of the services provided.

Underlying the stated objectives were a set of concerns about the management of public expenditure, the control of local authorities and the continued restructuring of housing tenure. The government sought to make savings via subsidy reductions, and to remove distortions in the pattern of public expenditure arising from flows between HRAs and other local authority accounts. The designers of the NFR were clearly motivated by a wish to reduce the flexibility of local authorities to pursue their own policies and to respond to local housing problems. The NFR was also shaped by a preference for non-municipal housing, and the government's objective was to establish a mechanism to reduce the attractiveness of council housing by higher rents and lower subsidies, together with tighter controls on capital resources available for improvement of existing houses.

There was considerable consultation with the local authority associations during 1988/89 and certain quite significant changes were made, but the basic principles outlined in the consultation paper were enshrined in the Act. The new system retains the principle of deficit subsidy and the notional HRA as the basis for the calculation of that subsidy. There are, however, several important changes.

Six of these changes should be highlighted. First, the NFR contains a major innovation in the form of the HRA subsidy. For almost 20 years councils had received a specific (earmarked) rent rebate subsidy which was separate from any general housing subsidy. The key differences between the two types of assistance were that general subsidy was dependent upon the notional deficit on the HRA whereas rebate subsidy was based on the actual rebate entitlement of all qualifying tenants and was really a form of social security rather than a housing subsidy. Nevertheless, the HRA subsidy combines these two elements in one deficit subsidy. The effect of adopting this approach was to expand the definition of what counts as the deficit on the HRA, thereby returning virtually all authorities to a situation in which they are vulnerable to leverage on rents by subsidy withdrawal.

Second, the HRA is now ring-fenced in the sense that authorities no longer have the power to make discretionary payments between the HRA and other accounts. This means that money paid into the HRA must be spent on housing services (or carried forward within the account for use in another year). However, when an authority reaches a position where it is no longer entitled to subsidy (ie when, in effect, net rent income equals or exceeds notional expenditure) then, under Section 80(2) of the 1989 Act, it is required to make specified transfers to the general fund equivalent to any overall negative subsidy entitlement. At this point the authority also acquires the freedom to make further discretionary payments from the HRA to the general fund.

Third, the NFR introduced differentiation of guideline rent increases and M&M allowances. The 1980 Act gave the secretary of state power to issue different determinations for different authorities but this was never done. Throughout the 1980s, the government issued standard annual determinations of the assumed increases in rents and M&M allowances, expressed in pounds per week for rents and percentages of annual expenditure for M&M allowances. Under the NFR, however, each authority receives a specific rent guideline and M&M allowance. The policy objectives underlying this approach are to do with a desire to produce a pattern of rents which is more closely related to local and regional variations in the value of property in the private sector, and to encourage a pattern of M&M spending which is related to differences in stock characteristics. It is important to remember that local authorities remain free to set the rents of individual dwellings, subject to the requirement that they have regard to private sector differentials for similar properties in the area.

Fourth, there are important changes in the treatment of receipts from the sale of council houses and housing land. Under the 1980 Act system, English authorities were constrained in their use of receipts to finance capital spending but were not required to use receipts to redeem debt. Interest on unspent receipts was credited to the HRA. Now authorities are required to set aside 75% of the receipts from council house sales, and 50% of those from land sales, against debt, and interest from the remaining 'usable' receipts is credited to the general fund. Given the operation of the subsidy system, authorities can no longer use interest from receipts to finance HRA spending (except for a small number of authorities which are now wholly debt-free).

Fifth, changes in debt charges are normally matched pound for pound in subsidy. Consequently, authorities receive no benefit from setting aside receipts since the net reduction in debt charges is matched by reduced subsidy. Conversely, the revenue effects of new capital spending receive 100% subsidy, compared with 75% under the 1980 Act system. In addition it should be noted that rent rebate expenditure is generally subsidisable at 100% within the HRA.

Sixth, the subsidy calculation under the NFR is based on what is referred to as a fundamental approach which involves a comparison of notional income and expenditure in the year, whereas under the 1980 Act the approach was incremental in the sense that the starting point was the subsidy received in the previous year. The decision to opt for the fundamental method was influenced by the transitional problems arising from the prohibition of rate fund contributions, and avoided complicated calculations about the value of such contributions.

Taken together these various elements produced a radically different environment for the management of local authority HRAs and significant changes in the presentation of the accounts. The ring-fence and the changes affecting the use of interest on capital receipts mean that authorities now have only one major source of income under their control: rents. This represents an important reduction in the flexibility of response available to local authorities in managing their finances. In terms of the way that the accounts are presented, the main change is that rent rebates now appear as an expenditure item, and on the income side rents are shown gross whereas previously they were shown net of rebates.

The introduction of the NFR did not necessarily imply a significant impact on rents and expenditure levels, and the DOE consultation paper said "it is essential ... that the introduction of the new system should not of itself introduce any sharp change in the level of rents or management and maintenance spending in any individual authority" (Department of the Environment, 1988, p 7). This is generally referred to as an attempt to produce a 'smooth landing'. The impact of the system depended very much on the rent and expenditure assumptions made by the DOE in the calculation of subsidy, the accuracy of the inflation assumptions and the quality of the data on local circumstances. The actual impact is discussed in Chapter 4, but first it is necessary to refer to the new arrangements for capital finance.

New arrangements for capital finance

The 1989 Act introduced measures designed to address problems inherited from the 1980s and to establish a framework for the distribution and control of capital resources in the future. The particular problems which emerged in the 1980s were the accumulation of capital receipts and the proliferation of schemes designed to exploit loopholes in the 1980 system. In the case of capital receipts, the 1989 Act required local authorities to set aside a fixed percentage (75% of receipts from the sale of houses and 50% of other receipts) for the redemption of debt, so that they are not available to finance capital expenditure in subsequent years. The various loopholes which had been developed by local authorities were blocked off by bringing them within the definition of 'credit arrangements'. In the new system, direct control over local authority capital expenditure is exercised through a system of 'credit approvals' which define the maximum amount of capital expenditure which may be financed in any year by borrowing or credit arrangements. Capital expenditure may also be financed from revenue or from 'usable' capital receipts, ie that proportion of receipts which is not required to be set aside for debt redemption. In determining the annual credit approval for an authority the government is now able to take into account the usable capital receipts available to the authority. This provides a mechanism for redressing the maldistribution of capital spending power produced by the old mechanism.

Each year every authority is given a HIP allocation which consists of an annual capital guideline (ACG) and an allocation for specified capital grants (SCGs). The SCG refers to expenditure on private sector renovation through the improvement grant system, and the ACG is broadly the amount available to be spent on the public sector stock (although authorities have discretion to use ACG resources to support the private sector programme, and/or non-housing capital expenditure).

The total amount of capital expenditure which may be financed by borrowing, the basic credit approval (BCA), is the sum of the SCG and the ACG minus a figure for receipts taken into account (RTIA):

BCA = (ACG - RTIA) + SCG

In addition to the BCA, local authorities may receive supplementary credit approvals (SCAs) for specific purposes. Authorities which have relatively low levels of assessed 'need to spend' plus relatively high reserves of capital receipts are most likely to be given a nil BCA. It is important to note that because capital expenditure is not ring-fenced each authority is given a single BCA figure covering all services. However, each authority is also given a specified amount which represents the maximum figure for housing capital expenditure which will be subsidisable within the HRA. Authorities are free to spend more of their BCA on housing, and to debit the debt charges to the HRA, but such expenditure would result in higher rents rather than higher subsidy.

The lack of a ring-fence around housing capital expenditure is an important feature of the new system. It means that there is scope for authorities to use housing credit approvals and housing capital receipts to fund non-housing expenditure, and vice versa. However, the housing subsidy system acts as a brake on the extent to which authorities are likely to redistribute expenditure.

Leverage

HRA subsidy payable to each authority under the NFR can be analysed as the sum of two elements:

● a housing element calculated as the surplus or deficit on a notional HRA where rents are set at the guideline and M&M spending equals the allowance: notional capital financing costs normally mirror actual costs;

● a rent rebate element which closely reflects actual rent rebate spending.

The rent rebate element will always be a positive amount, but the housing element will be positive when the notional HRA shows a deficit and negative when it shows a surplus. If the notional surplus is greater than the rent rebate subsidy entitlement, the authority has, in effect, a negative entitlement to HRA subsidy and is required to transfer at least that amount out of the HRA.

Since local authorities are not required to set rents equal to guidelines, or M&M spending equal to allowances, it is necessary to consider how year-on-year changes in subsidy entitlement are likely to affect budget-setting behaviour. An authority can normally assume that subsidy will reflect actual changes in capital financing costs and rent rebate spending, and consequently these aspects of the subsidy determination are unlikely to affect its budgeting behaviour. The crucial elements in the subsidy determination are the guideline rent and the M&M allowance. The difference between them - that is, the amount of subsidy withdrawn, abstracting from changes in capital financing costs and rent rebate subsidy - is a measure of the leverage exerted on authorities by the subsidy system.

In each of the three years of the NFR, the DOE has increased the average guideline rent by more than the average M&M allowance. Comparing 1992/93 with 1989/90, the average guideline rent is £6.36 per week higher (£331 per year) but the average M&M allowance only £150 per year higher, resulting in an average leverage of £181 per dwelling over the first three years of the NFR.

The leverage on an individual authority can, however, vary considerably depending on the pre-NFR rent, the value of the authority's stock and whether or not it has benefited from M&M targeting. Among the case study authorities leverage varied from £6 (Rhymney Valley) to £476 (Cotswold).

The same leverage can be produced by an indefinite number of pairings of changes in rent guidelines and M&M allowances intended to send the authority very different policy signals. For example, the maximum guideline rent increase, coupled with substantial benefit from targeting, may exert the same leverage on an authority as the minimum guideline rent increase coupled with the minimum uplift in the M&M allowance. But in the first case the government's intention is that the authority should increase both rents and spending substantially, and in the second that it should contain spending and rents. Yet, unless DOE guidelines and allowances in themselves carry weight in local budget deliberations there is no pressure on authorities to behave in one way rather than another. Given that one of the government's objections to the 1980 Act system was that it allowed certain authorities to operate a low-rent, low-spending policy, it is noteworthy that the NFR seems to impose little incentive to depart from such a policy.

Discussion

The 1989 Act laid down the basic framework of the NFR but the impact of the new regime on local authorities has been dependent on the annual subsidy determinations issued by the DOE and, in particular, on the rent guidelines and M&M allowances contained in those determinations.

In introducing the NFR, the government was explicitly committed to raising rents generally and to increasing rent differentials between authorities with high and low valued stock. The government's objective in relation to M&M spending was less clearly stated, but there were suggestions that some authorities at least should be encouraged to spend more on management and maintenance to finance better services to tenants. However, these objectives have not been addressed through rent guidelines which, for example, reflect a particular gross rate of return on estimated stock values, or M&M allowances which reflect estimates of authorities' need to spend. The annual subsidy determination is an output from the public expenditure round and, in consequence, reflects assumptions about the appropriate level of spending on management and maintenance and about aggregate rents at the national level. Rent guidelines and M&M allowances at the individual local authority level are calculated by way of formally distributing the national aggregates for rents and M&M spending. In determining the national aggregates, the government faces a trade off between the level of rent guidelines and M&M allowances. Consistent with any given level of intended public expenditure, there is an indefinite number of pairings of rent and expenditure levels. However, in determining the extent to which it is prepared to impose higher rent guidelines in order to finance higher levels of expenditure on management and maintenance, the government must have regard to the fact that, at the margin, 70% of rent income is met from housing benefit.

Progress towards the government's rent and expenditure objectives has also been constrained by the commitment to a 'smooth landing' given before the NFR was introduced. Hence the government has seen it as necessary to constrain progression towards rent guidelines which fully reflect stock values by 'damping': imposing a maximum guideline rent increase and, in order that the aggregate guideline rent income is not thereby reduced, a minimum guideline increase as well. Authorities with low stock values have been given higher rent guidelines to compensate for lower rent guidelines in the high value authorities. Progression towards target M&M allowances has also been constrained by the commitment to a smooth landing. In practice, this has meant that commitments have been given to limit the reductions in allowances for those authorities whose target allowances are below the historic level of real expenditure on management and maintenance. But meeting this commitment within a limited aggregate allowance means that authorities which stand to benefit from target allowances have not yet seen their allowances increased to target levels.

three

OPERATING THE NEW FINANCIAL REGIME

The implementation of housing policy in Britain is conventionally seen as a local level activity in which central government sets the legislative framework but local authorities actually carry out the work of providing houses, improvement grants and so forth (Malpass and Murie, 1990, p 10; Houlihan, 1988). In the case of the NFR, however, central government has an important implementation role to play, and it is reasonable to think in terms of the DOE and the Welsh Office (WO) implementing the system rather than the local authorities. The NFR is a policy instrument which is designed to be operated by the DOE and WO on an annual basis, and in this sense it is quite different from, for example, the right to buy which was designed to be implemented at the local level as councils responded to tenants' applications to buy their homes. In the case of the right to buy, once the legislation was put in place the role of the centre was largely confined to monitoring or policing the local authority response, although this has been interpreted as the DOE taking an active role in implementation (Forrest and Murie, 1985, p 30). The involvement of the DOE and WO in the implementation of the NFR is much more than a policing role; the central departments are responsible for a crucial set of inputs each year, the specification of which has a considerable impact on the pattern of policy outcomes.

The annual round

The implementation of the NFR is based on an annual cycle of bidding, budgeting, spending and accounting. The cycle begins in May each year when, very early in the financial year, central government departments make their bids for spending in the next financial year. This is the beginning of the PESC (Public Expenditure Survey Committee) process in which the Treasury negotiates with the spending departments the volume of public expenditure and its distribution. Within the DOE, bids pass up from the specialists in the various sections to be amalgamated in one aggregate bid for housing. In the case of housing revenue, considerations which would influence the bid might include forecasting adjustments arising from, for example, increased claims for housing benefit. Other influences on the bid would include DOE aspirations to move the subsidy system in particular directions: to extend the targeting of M&M allowances or to raise rents in real terms. Civil servants can, at this stage, bid for a budget which is neutral in terms of public expenditure or which implies changes in either direction. It would be misleading to think of the NFR as being entirely driven by public expenditure considerations; there remain objectives concerned with the incentives given to local authorities and the preference for a simplified system.

In the years under consideration the PESC process involved a series of 'bi-laterals' or meetings between individual departments and the Treasury, the outcome of which was to give, by about September, some indication of the level of resources that would be available in the next financial year. Within the DOE there was then a top-down distribution of the resources, reflecting the bottom-up bidding process earlier in the year.

The 1989 Act requires the DOE/WO to consult the local authority associations on draft proposals for the next financial year and to make the first determination, covering rent guidelines, M&M allowances and admissible credit approvals, available by Christmas. In practice officials are in regular contact with their counterparts in the AMA, ADC and Council of Welsh Districts (CWD) throughout the year, and they aspire to resolve most contentious issues in advance of the formal consultation period. Ministers are also directly involved in determining the changes in guideline rents and M&M allowances, and are required by Section 80 of the 1989 Act to have regard to past and expected movements in prices and incomes as well as other factors.

Once the determinations have been sent out to local authorities the focus of attention shifts to the local level as authorities make their rent increase decisions in January and February. This is in order to comply with the requirement to set the HRA budget by the end of February and in time to give tenants four weeks' notice before implementing any increase from April.

In parallel with the preparations for the next financial year, the DOE/WO is involved in monitoring the subsidy claim forms submitted by local authorities during the year. Claims are made on four successive sets of forms, known as 'first advance', 'second advance', 'pre-audit final' and 'audit final'. Auditing of local authority accounts, on which final claims are based, takes place some months after the end of the financial year. The result is that the DOE/WO becomes involved in resolving problems with those accounts at a much later date; during the summer of 1992 officials were working on the audited accounts for 1990/91. Thus, although there is a clear annual rhythm to the implementation of the NFR, the activities of the DOE/WO officials during the year embrace planning for next year, monitoring the current year and concluding business from previous years.

Having outlined the main stages and activities during the year it is now necessary to turn to a discussion of the way the NFR has been implemented so far. The first point to make here is that the policy-making and implementation timetable in 1988/89 and 1990/91 was very tight with the result that some aspects of the system, notably the specification of the ring-fence and the targeting of M&M allowances, were not ready for the April 1990 start. In these circumstances it was perhaps difficult for the designers to anticipate the implementation problems which later emerged.

Rent guidelines

In order to achieve the objective of local authority rents which more closely reflect local and regional variations in property values, the NFR incorporates a new system for setting guideline rents for each authority each year. The rent guidelines set for the first three years of the NFR are shown in Table 1. These are derived by a procedure which begins from an 'assumed national rent', and calculates notional rents for each authority on the principle that each authority's contribution to the assumed national rent should be proportional to the capital value of its housing stock, estimated from recent right to buy prices (before discount). These notional rents are then compared with the previous year's guideline rents. In each of the three years of the system the implied increases have been very large in some authorities, mainly in London and the

South East, while in others the comparison implies a rent reduction. Each year, accordingly, the DOE/WO has damped the rent guidelines by specifying a maximum and a minimum increase over the previous year's guideline, or, in the first year, 1990/91, over actual rents in 1989/90. Damping works by redistribution: authorities whose rents already exceed those implied by local property values are nevertheless given guideline increases in order to reduce the guideline increases in authorities where rents are well below the levels implied by property values.

Table 1:   DOE rent assumptions, 1990/91 to 1992/93

		1990/91	1991/92	1992/93
Minimum guideline increase				
	England	£0.95	£1.38	£1.20
	Wales	£1.05	£1.35	£1.13
Maximum guideline increase				
	England	£4.50	£2.50	£4.50
	Wales	£3.15	£2.73	£3.40
Average guideline increase				
	England	£2.08	£1.84	£2.44
	Wales	£1.54	£1.88	£2.12
Average guideline rent				
	England	£23.06	£24.90	£27.31
	Wales	£22.93	£24.72	£26.85
Inflation assumption		5.0%	6.0%	4.5%
Real increase				
	England	5.0%	2.0%	5.0%
	Wales	2.0%	2.0%	4.0%

Source: DOE and WO

There is a very marked regional pattern to the distribution of guideline rent increases. In 1990/91, 43% of all English authorities were given the minimum guideline, but in the three northern regions 88% of authorities were in this position. In 1991/92 more authorities were at either the top or bottom of the range, but 90% of northern authorities were at the bottom while 82% of authorities in

London, the South East and eastern region were at the top. In 1992/93 all 36 metropolitan authorities were on the minimum guideline of £1.20, together with 76 non-metropolitan districts, only three of which could be defined as being in the South. Meanwhile, of 71 authorities given the maximum £4.50, 15 were in London and none north of Cambridge. Thus most northern authorities have been assumed to raise rents by just £3.53 in three years, while in some southern authorities the notional aggregate increase amounts to £11.50.

Management and maintenance allowances

Alongside rent guidelines which reflect variations in the capital value of each local authority's stock, the government's objective is to differentiate M&M allowances in the subsidy calculation to reflect variations in the need to spend on the stock. However, in discussions between central government officials and the local authority associations during 1989, it proved impossible to reach agreement on a method of measuring variations in the need to spend. For 1990/91 each authority's allowance was calculated from the average of its actual M&M spending in the three years 1986/87 to 1988/89 uplifted to 1989/90 prices, or notional spending in 1989/90, whichever was the greater. This amount was increased by 8% to produce allowances for 1990/91 which were said to allow for a 3% real increase in spending.

However, for some authorities, specifically those which had been capitalising repairs, the provisional allowances were significantly below actual expenditure in previous years. Lobbying of the DOE by the AMA on behalf of member authorities such as North Tyneside (see Chapter 5) produced a response which involved the introduction of a set of 'regional floor' M&M allowances. The effect of this concession was to increase the aggregate M&M allowance by no more than 1% and to provide assistance for just 32 authorities, half of which were in the three northern regions. Although the aggregate effect was small the benefit to individual authorities was sometimes significant: North Tyneside's allowance rose from £293 to £508.

For 1991/92 the DOE developed a method, based on stock characteristics, of calculating targeted allowances for spending on repairs and maintenance (together with caretaking, cleaning, lighting and lifts) but not management. However, it worked by redistributing an aggregate national allowance which, for 1991/92 represented a 6% increase on the aggregate allowance for 1990/91 allowing no real increase in spending. Consequently, authorities could only gain from targeting at the expense of others losing. Progress towards targeted allowances in England was confined to the 44 authorities whose 1990/91 allowances were more than £120 below their targets, at the expense of 36 authorities whose 1990/91 targets were more than £160 above their targets and whose 1991/92 allowances were thus frozen at their 1990/91 levels. All the other authorities in England received the 1990/91 maintenance allowance increased by 5.5% (0.5% less than the predicted rate of inflation). Eighteen of the gainers were in London and the remainder were evenly spread through the regions. Of the losers, 27 were in the South and 9 in the North. Management allowances were simply the 1990/91 allowances increased by 6%. The WO developed its own, slightly different, method of targeting, using the Welsh House Condition Survey as a key source of data on stock condition.

In 1992/93 target allowances for each authority in England (but not in Wales) included management as well as maintenance. The aggregate allowance was increased by 6.5% (predicted to be 2% in real terms). All authorities received a minimum increase of 3.5% (a 1% cut in real terms) and the 135 authorities in England whose target allowances were more than this amount received an additional allowance equal to 31.5% of the difference.

The system in operation

In each of the three years of the NFR, most authorities have increased rents by significantly more than the guideline increases. Since 1989/90, average rents in England have risen by 47% compared with a guideline increase of 30%. Table 2 shows that rents have also risen significantly relative to average earnings. Between 1983 and 1988 this ratio had been falling slowly, although between 1980 and 1982 there had been a much steeper rise from 6% to over 8% (Hills, 1991, pp 38-40).

Table 2:   Actual and guideline rents 1989/90 to 1992/93 (England)

	1989/90	1990/91	1991/92	1992/93
DOE guideline rent (£ pw)	20.97	23.05	24.89	27.33
Average actual rent (£ pw)	20.70	23.76	27.25	30.55
Average rent as % of earnings	7.6%	7.9%	8.4%	8.9%

Source: DOE

Most of the divergence of actual rents from guidelines is explained by expenditure on management and maintenance in excess of the allowances.   DOE figures suggest that average local authority budgeted M&M spending in England in 1992/93 was 13.3% above the average allowance: £965 per dwelling compared with an average allowance of £837.   This confirmed a trend which was apparent in the first two years of the NFR (Association of District Councils, 1990; 1991; Association of Metropolitan Authorities, 1990; 1991).

The other major contributory factor identified in the AMA and ADC surveys is a tendency for authorities to finance an increasing amount of capital outlay from rent income.   The AMA and ADC estimate that local authority budgets include increasing amounts for revenue contribution to capital outlay (RCCO), rising from £120 million in 1990/91 to £234 million in 1991/92 and to £278 million in 1992/93 (subsequent figures collected by the DOE suggest even higher levels of RCCO). Average rent increases would have been higher had not authorities also reduced the average year-end working balance in each of these years. These issues are discussed further in Chapter 4.

The DOE's target allowances for management and maintenance reflect its judgement of authorities' need to spend, within a constrained national aggregate allowance, rather than a judgement about their actual (absolute) need to spend. The national aggregate allowance remains linked to the aggregate of authorities' actual spending in the base years 1986/87 to 1988/89. There have been real increases in the aggregate allowance in two of the three years of the NFR, but in each case these appear to have been made to help honour the government's commitment to a soft landing for authorities in the transition to the NFR.   This is after representations from the local authority associations that some authorities would need to increase repairs spending financed from revenue to compensate for the reduced scope to capitalise repairs under the new capital rules. The 2% increase in 1992/93 was made to permit progress towards targeted allowances while reducing the scale of losses to authorities not benefiting from targeting.

While it is plausible that increases in actual spending reflect a real increasing need to spend, quantification of the need to spend presents considerable difficulty, particularly in relation to management (Jackson and Kleinman, 1992; Price Waterhouse, 1992). The DOE has never publicly expressed the view that the target M&M allowances reflect an objective calculation of the need to spend based on an implicit standard of service and the costs of providing it, allowing for changes in the degree of difficulty of the management task, the ageing and deterioration of the stock and other factors. Neither has the government made a statement about the efficiency savings which might be made on a year-to-year basis. Instead the DOE has tended to resist demands that allowances should be based on absolute, rather than relative, need to spend stressing that, in the end, the national aggregate allowance emerges from negotiations with the Treasury about the acceptable level of public expenditure. Within a given level of subsidy provision, the DOE faces a trade-off between the level of allowances and the rent guidelines. Ministers appear to give greater priority to guideline rent increases than to M&M allowances, and in a context where there is pressure to reduce subsidy without resort to politically risky rent increases there will continue to be a resistance to real increases in M&M allowances. However, the assumption of an underlying constant real need to spend is unrealistic. As argued above, expenditure on supervision and management was rising in real terms during the first half of the 1980s, and between 1987/88 and 1992/93 this trend continued, as is shown in more detail in the next chapter. Revenue expenditure per dwelling on both repair and maintenance, and supervision and management continues to increase in real terms, but total expenditure on repair and maintenance has been affected by the reduction in capitalised repairs since the introduction of the NFR.

Government control over subsidy paid

The total amount of subsidy payable nationally depends on three factors:

● the relationship between the assumed national rent and aggregate allowance for management and maintenance;

● changes in capital financing costs dependent on changes in interest rates and the relationship between new borrowing for HRA capital spending and capital receipts set aside against HRA debt;

● changes in rent rebate spending dependent on rent levels and changes in entitlement caused by fluctuations in incomes and unemployment.

DOE officials responsible for the operation of the NFR have control over only some of these variables: the assumed national rent and aggregate allowance for management and maintenance, and the level of capital allocations. Since authorities are free to transfer capital allocations between services, there is no direct control over housing capital spending. Interest rates and capital receipts are largely dependent on changes in the wider economy, rent rebate spending on similar changes and also on local authorities' actual rent increase decisions, not on guideline rents.

Although the assumed national rent has increased faster than the national aggregate allowance for management and maintenance, and net HRA debt has fallen, HRA subsidy provision has risen overall because of increased rent rebate spending. Further, because the public expenditure provision made for HRA subsidy was based on the assumption that local authorities would apply the guideline rent increases, the additional rebates payable (because rent increases have exceeded the guidelines) contributed to HRA subsidy exceeding the provision in both 1990/91 and 1991/92.

In terms of problems which emerged within central government it is appropriate to mention the difficulties generated by combining housing subsidy and rent rebate subsidy. Whereas during the 1980s the cost of housing benefit was accounted for within the social security budget, since 1990/91 the rent rebate costs of English local authority tenants fall within the DOE budget. The Department of Social Security (DSS) retains policy responsibility for the rules on rent rebate subsidy, but the DOE/WO is accountable for expenditure. This is seen to generate what one civil servant in the

DOE described as "all sorts of problems". The arrangement clearly puts considerable pressure on the DOE and DSS to cooperate and to maintain a close working relationship. The DOE perspective suggests that the DSS is primarily concerned with control of expenditure on rebates.

As indicated earlier, the DOE also has to negotiate with the Treasury, which is similarly concerned about containing expenditure levels. Given the Treasury's wish to reduce public expenditure, its contribution to the debate is to argue for higher rents and lower subsidy. So far, its point of view has been that the benefits of higher rents outweigh any impact that this has on inflation (a 1% increase in council rents is equivalent to only about 0.02% on the retail price index (RPI)). The Treasury is also concerned to make sure that spending departments stay within agreed budgets and in the first two years of the NFR this proved to be impossible. In 1990/91 the DOE had to seek a supplementary estimate of over £500 million (the largest supplementary estimate for any department since the costs of the Falklands War in 1982) and in 1991/92 the figure was £200 million. In the first year the main causes of the cost overrun were, first, the unanticipated increase in the cost of private sector leasing fuelled by the collapse of the property market and local authority exploitation of an opportunity to improve services for homeless families, and second, the resolution of matters relating to previous years. The higher than anticipated cost of rent rebates accounted for only about £75 million of the overrun in that year, but in 1991/92 rebate costs accounted for the majority of the overrun.

One of the problems for the DOE/WO is that they have to budget for a given level of rent increase, but in the knowledge that local authorities may implement increases above that level with knock-on effects in terms of rent rebate expenditure. This is clearly a major cause of debate and tension between the departments and the Treasury. The consequence of a cost overrun in one year is that the Treasury will try to recoup that expenditure in the next year by insisting on a large rent increase and/or a squeeze on M&M allowances, thereby reducing subsidy. The effect of this sort of Treasury pressure is to reduce the departments' capacity to extend the targeting of M&M resources.

One other point to mention here is that the NFR has proved to be, in the words of a DOE official, "hideously complicated", for both the centre and the local authorities. From the DOE point of view the system is complicated in the sense that there are complex interactions amongst different parts of the system embracing housing capital and revenue and the general fund. This means that fine-tuning the system is very complicated and more complicated than had been envisaged at the design stage. The DOE perception by mid 1992 was that the evidence from the audited accounts of 1990/91 showed that local authorities had also found the system very hard to understand and operate properly. It was also clear that the auditors had themselves struggled with the new system. In contrast to the administration of the capital side of housing finance, where the DOE regional offices play a significant role, the complexity of the revenue side is seen to preclude regional office involvement thereby placing all the burden on staff at DOE headquarters on Marsham Street. Part of the difficulty of operating the NFR is that it is an inherently complex data-based system which requires local authorities to produce huge amounts of information; the first advance subsidy claim form for 1991/92, for example, ran to 24 pages and contained 790 cells. In the transitional phase many authorities found themselves in the position of having to generate statistics which were not routinely available, or which were not reliable because under the 1980 system they had not been in receipt of subsidy.

four

PATTERNS OF IMPACT AND RESPONSE

Introduction

The purpose of this chapter is to give a general and quantified description of the impact of the NFR at regional and local level. It also provides a picture of the general pattern of responses of local authorities to the new system, and begins to provide some explanation for the more systematic patterns of response through the use of statistical techniques. The evidence which emerges confirms a rather mixed picture in terms of achievement of the objectives of the system.

The chapter draws on an analysis of statistical data referring to the 366 local housing authorities in England. More details on the data sources and some more detailed tables of results are included in the appendix to this chapter (see p 64).

The descriptive tables and charts break local authorities down in three ways: (i) London/metropolitan/non-metropolitan class; (ii) four broad regions; (iii) type of area using the Shaw classification (see appendix). Other classifying variables, for example size and political control, are used in the statistical analysis reported near the end of the chapter.

The data describe the medium-term effects of the NFR on rents, expenditure and subsidy taking the period from 1987/88 to 1991/92 (or 1992/93 where possible). This complements other published analyses, for example the annual ADC/AMA surveys, which tend to concentrate on one year's changes. There are other reasons for this medium-term perspective as well. The transition to the new system was complex and involved some important one-off rules and decisions which favoured certain types of local situation and ignored or disfavoured others. It is important to include these transitional effects as well as the effects of the new system operating in its more normal mode. In addition, it is widely recognised that many local authorities engaged in anticipatory behaviour, both real changes (eg spending more on capitalised repairs) and accounting changes. These decisions had a strong effect on the financial year 1989/90 as well as some effects on the years immediately before and after. This is a further good reason to focus on changes from the 'before' situation of 1987 to the 'after' of 1991 or 1992. Lastly, 1987/88 effectively pre-dates all of the major changes in housing ushered in by the 1987 White Paper.

The broad patterns of change

The bar charts in Figures 1-7 in this section provide a clear picture for the main variables of interest over the transition period. They also indicate divergences between the collective behaviour of local authorities and the official guidelines issued by the DOE.

The figures are coded as described below:

L	London
M	Metropolitan
NM	Non-metropolitan
IC	Inner city
RC	Regional centre
DI	Declining industrial
AS	Affluent suburb
G	Growing
R	Rural
R&C	Resort and coastal
N	North
MI	Midlands
S	South
E	England

Rents

As already seen in Chapter 3, rents have risen sharply on average at well above the general inflation rate. Average rents in 1992 were 71% above 1987 levels, a rate of increase nearly double the 37%

rise in general inflation (RPI) and well above the 49% rise in average earnings.

Figure 1 shows clearly how the rise was much larger in absolute and percentage terms in London and the South. For example, the data collected showed that London rents rose from £20.00 to £41.00 per week, an increase of 105%, and the corresponding figures for the South East were from under £19.00 to nearly £36.00, an increase of 88%. By contrast, rents in Yorkshire and Humberside rose from under £17.00 to only £23.50, a more modest rise of only 39% which about equates with the rate of general inflation and is less than the increase in earnings.

These contrasts show that in certain respects averages can mislead. Perhaps more important than the national average increase in rents has been the large difference in impact between different parts of the country, principally between north and south.

A consequence of this is that whereas in 1987 one could say that council rents varied relatively little between different regions of the country, in 1992 the variation is quite marked (again, this point is brought out by Figure 1). Average London rents were only 23% above rents in the northern regions in 1987, but by 1992 they were 68% higher. This is a direct consequence of the policy intentions of the government which were that council rents should in future bear a closer relationship to market values and rents. This aim has already been achieved to a substantial measure despite the damping of guideline rent increases. For example, comparing Nationwde Building Society prices for semi-detached houses in 1992, London prices averaged 82% higher than the North, compared with 68% higher for council rents. However, in the South East prices averaged 41% higher than the North compared with 45% for council rents. This, of course, is at a time of extreme recession in the housing market, most especially in the South East. In most of recent history the differences between values in the South and the North have been greater than they have been since 1990. For example, in early 1987 South East prices were 125% higher than those in the North. On the other hand, market rents in the small private rented sector have actually varied less than capital values, which suggests again that the NFR is coming close to its general aim.

Figure 1 reveals that the sharp rise in rents occurred in all the main types of district characteristic of the non-metropolitan South: the affluent suburbs, growth areas, rural districts and resort/coastal areas. The differentiation is mainly determined by region.

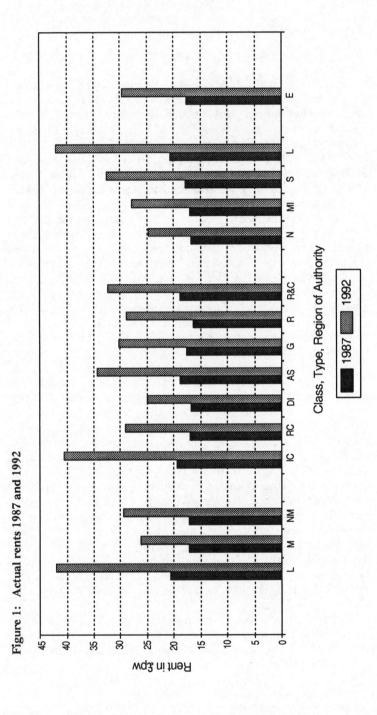

Figure 1: Actual rents 1987 and 1992

Rent in £pw

Class, Type, Region of Authority

1987 1992

Average rents are now over guideline levels in all regions and types of area (Figure 2). The margin is greatest in London and least in the North and in declining industrial areas, but the general tendency to exceed guidelines is apparent everywhere. Chapter 2 explained the logic of the NFR subsidy system, that rents deviate from guidelines where expenditure on management and maintenance exceeds allowances or where capital is funded from revenue (RCCOs), although other factors (mainly transitional) can also cause such discrepancies. Thus, the main reason for these higher-than-guideline rents is the higher-than-allowance M&M expenditure, discussed further below.

Repair and maintenance

As argued earlier, one intention of the NFR was to improve the performance of local authorities in managing and maintaining their stock. The last chapter discussed overall spending on management and maintenance. In this chapter, repairs and maintenance are considered separately from supervision and management, and account is taken of capital expenditure. How has the introduction of the NFR affected expenditure on repair and maintenance?

Figures 3 and 4 provide a revealing comparison of expenditure on this aspect of the housing service between 1987/88 and 1991/92. The figures are in real terms (assuming RPI approximately reflects inflation in repair and maintenance costs) and include revenue expenditure, RCCOs and capitalised repairs funded in other ways. These are mainly from capital receipts (capital spending is estimated from the average spend in the two years 1987/88 and 1988/89, to reduce the lumpiness of data for a single year).

The picture for 1987/88 is very striking, showing as it does a very heavy reliance on capitalised repairs. It was possible to fund repairs from capital receipts outside the capital control system at that time. In some areas, notably London and metropolitan areas, the majority of repair activity was being funded in this way in 1987/88. The effect of the new capital control system, restricting the use of capital receipts to 25% and a much reduced total of receipts in the housing slump, is that there has been a massive overall reduction in repair and maintenance spending on the council stock. The scale of the reduction is as much as 57% in London, and averages 23% overall. Local authorities are pushing their rents up beyond guidelines and increasing RCCOs, but Figure 4 makes clear that this is an inadequate substitute for the lost capital spending.

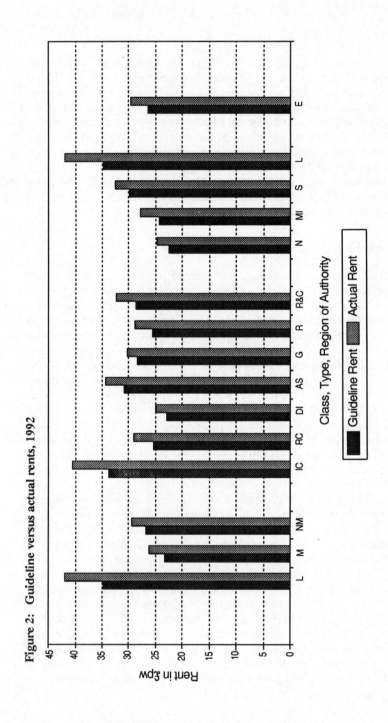

Figure 2: Guideline versus actual rents, 1992

Rent in £pw

Class, Type, Region of Authority

Guideline Rent   Actual Rent

Figure 3: Repairs and maintenance expenditure, 1987/88 (@ 1991 prices)

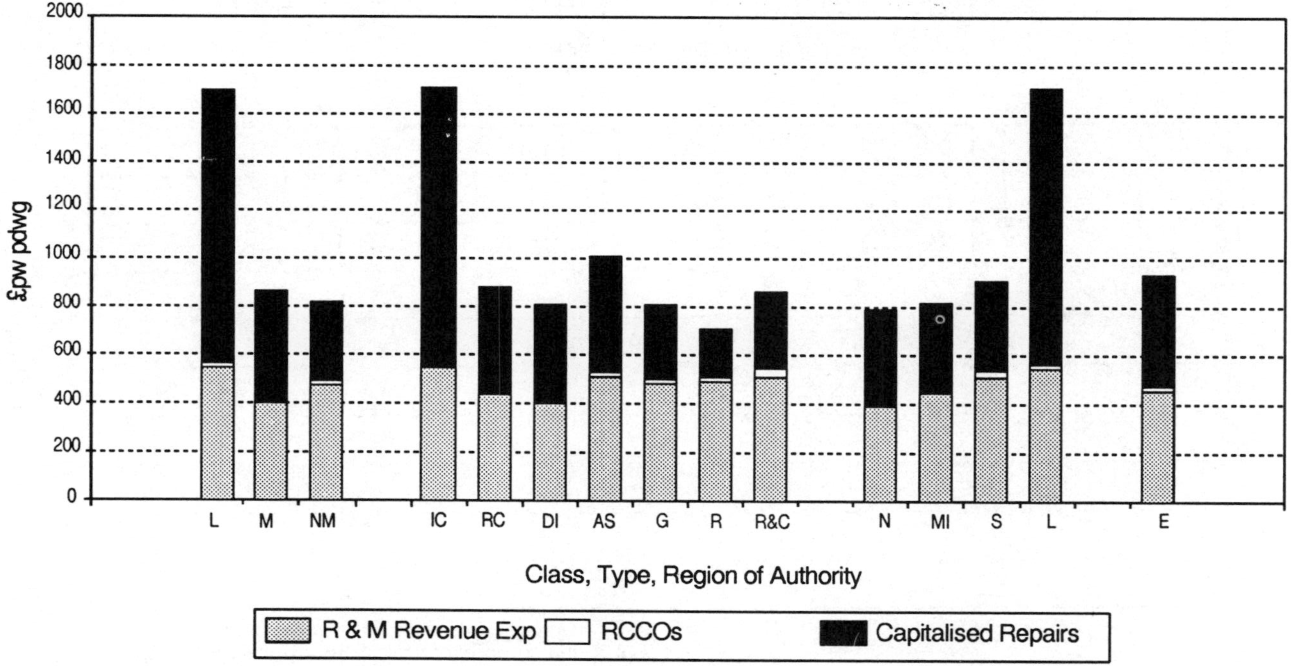

Figure 4: Repairs and maintenance expenditure, 1991/92

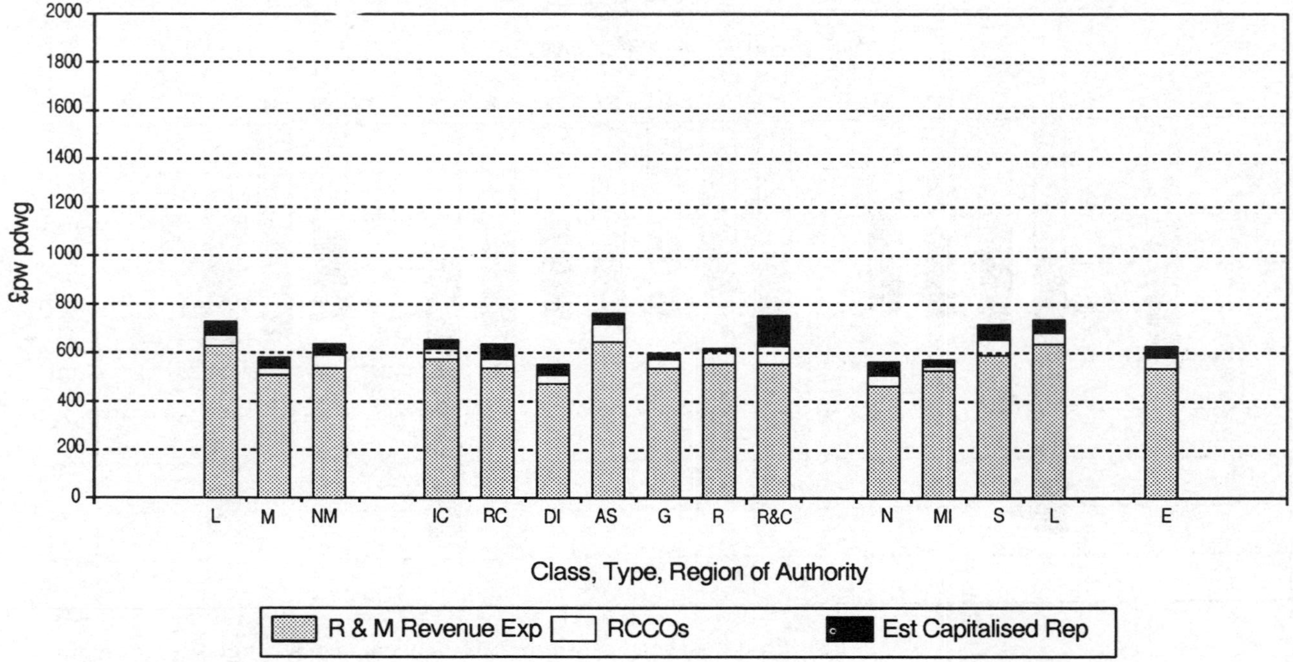

While the high spending in the 1988/90 period may well have reduced the scale of backlog disrepair in council housing, it is questionable whether the current reduced rate is sufficient to even maintain the stock in a constant, unsatisfactory condition (Audit Commission, 1992). In this sense, the outcome of the new system seems to be in conflict with one of its general stated aims. It is an outcome which was foreseen and subject of much lobbying at the time of the introduction of the new system, and the government chose not to respond to the representations of the AMA, LBA and ALA on this issue.

While rents have become increasingly differentiated, spending levels on repair and maintenance have moved toward a more uniform pattern, comparing Figures 3 and 4. The biggest cutbacks have been in London and other inner-city areas, and metropolitan areas as a whole have seen much more reduction than non-metropolitan areas. The least severe reductions tend to be in the non-metropolitan South, including rural and resort/coastal areas. In 1991/92 the level of expenditure per dwelling varies much less than in 1987/88 across regions and types. The type of district with the highest expenditure per unit now is the affluent suburb, followed by the resort/coastal district; the type with the lowest spending is the declining industrial area. Intuitively, one would have to say that this pattern is the opposite of what one would expect on the basis of targeting resources on areas of greatest need, the supposed objective of the NFR. For example, comparing metropolitan and non-metropolitan areas within regions, it is generally true that metropolitan areas have higher estimated backlog repairs.

A further test of this issue is to calculate the correlation coefficient between two indicators of the need to spend and actual spending per dwelling in 1987/88 and in 1991/92. The two indicators are (i) a best estimate of the cost of backlog repairs for each authority, and (ii) the undamped target for recurrent repair and maintenance spending in 1992. This shows that in neither year was there a significant correlation between backlog repairs and total spending (the correlation coefficients are -0.039 and 0.017 respectively). There was quite a strong relationship between spending and the second need indicator, the undamped target (which is supposed to represent the need for ongoing programmed maintenance) in 1987/88, but this was much weaker in 1991/92 (the correlation coefficients are 0.69 and 0.19 respectively). This particular test suggests that expenditure on repair and maintenance was more effectively targeted in 1987/88 than under the NFR in

1991/92. It also suggests that the targeting, such as it is, does not relate at all to backlog repairs. The measure of backlog repairs is based on very inadequate proxy information (although this includes the DOE's official index and the local authorities' own estimates) so one cannot put too much weight on this evidence alone, but taken in conjunction with the patterns described above it does give a rather strong message.

We can only conclude, on this important aspect of policy, that the NFR has clearly failed in meeting its stated objective. Spending on the council housing stock has dropped steeply and is less well targeted on areas of need than before.

Supervision and management

The picture with respect to supervision and management expenditure revealed by Figure 5 is quite different. This expenditure, which all falls directly on the revenue account, has increased strongly in all areas. This is a real terms increase, adjusting for inflation using the RPI, although it is arguable that in such a labour-intensive activity a different index such as earnings might be more appropriate. The sheer size of the average increase, 64% in cash, 25% over RPI, is noteworthy in its own right. These figures imply an annual average real rate of growth of 5.7% over the period. This confirms a trend established in the early 1980s. The possible reasons for this were discussed in Chapter 1.

Has the NFR in any way contributed to this growth in real spending? It is difficult to see how the NFR is directly responsible as the growth pre-dates it by a decade. However, it could be argued that the NFR has changed the climate for local decision making on both rents and expenditure. In the past, rent increases and expectations of rent levels were low; to argue for large rent and service increases would have been to step out of line. With the new regime, rents have to rise substantially in most areas for reasons that are largely beyond the control of authorities. Expectations of rent levels have changed. In this context, some further increase to finance a better service becomes easier to contemplate. The converse may also apply; high rents may mean that tenants will no longer tolerate a poor service. These points are speculative. Local decision making on rents and spending is discussed further in the next chapter.

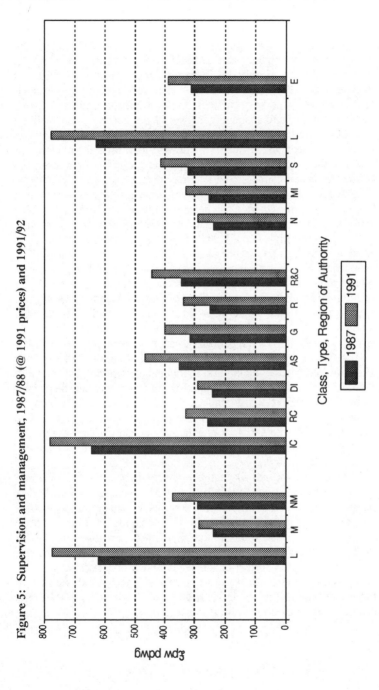

Figure 5: Supervision and management, 1987/88 (@ 1991 prices) and 1991/92

While government policy aims have clearly included the achievement of higher standards of service from management, whether this can simply be interpreted as higher expenditure is questionable. The expectation must also have been of higher cost-effectiveness. It is very difficult to say what the optimal balance between repairs and management would be, but it is very striking that there should be such a large discrepancy between spending on these two aspects of service. This does at least raise the question of whether the impact of the new system will improve or worsen the balance between management and maintenance activity.

The level of housing management expenditure was very much higher in London than elsewhere in both years (Figure 5). This reflects at least in part the interaction of more difficult to manage stock (eg more high density flatted property), more problems such as rent arrears, and higher labour and other input costs. The proportional rate of increase was actually higher for non-metropolitan districts (20%) than for the London boroughs (16%) or the metropolitan authorities (11%). Outside London, the highest spending continues to be in affluent suburbs and resort/coastal districts. Again, one might question the extent to which this pattern is a good reflection of the pattern of needs or problems.

Local authorities are spending significantly over their allowances for management and maintenance together, by 13.3% in 1992/93. As discussed in the previous chapter, this can be argued to be an indication of the inadequacy of the allowance relative to what local authorities collectively believe they need to spend. The average level of the allowances is heavily constrained by the public expenditure planning control totals because higher allowances mean higher subsidy.

Figure 6 shows that the pattern of spending across regions and types of area is similar to the pattern of allowances, but at a higher general level. This might be taken as evidence of successful targeting, but such a conclusion would not be justified. Apart from London, it is difficult to argue that the pattern of allowances shown in Figure 6 (eg higher in non-metropolitan areas and affluent suburbs) is a good reflection of needs and problems. In fact, the damped allowances are mainly determined by past expenditure in the years leading up to the introduction of the NFR. Thus, the relationship with expenditure is unsurprising.

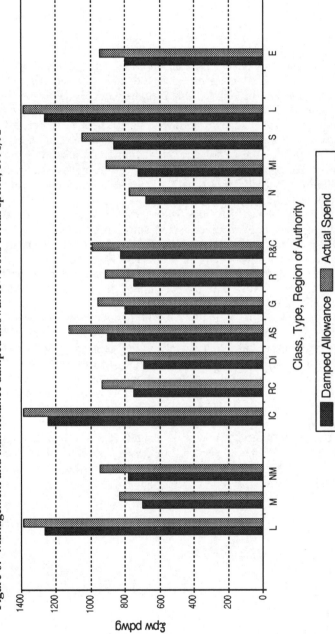

Figure 6: Management and maintenance damped allowance versus actual spend, 1991/92

Subsidy

Housing subsidy is defined, as described in Chapter 2, as the general housing element of subsidy to the HRA excluding rent rebate subsidy. In 1987/88 this included both Exchequer subsidy and rate fund contributions, with transfers from the HRA to the rate fund treated as negative subsidy. In 1991/92 it is defined as "housing revenue account subsidy minus rent rebates", and this figure can often be negative. This definition of subsidy is a cash flow type of definition based on the historic cost accounting definitions of the HRA; it is not the same as an economic definition of subsidy (Bramley, 1991).

Figure 7 shows that subsidy in 1987/88 was concentrated in London, with only relatively small amounts on average going to metropolitan and non-metropolitan districts (most received no Exchequer subsidy). Only in a minority of authorities, typically affluent suburbs and resort/coastal areas had local authorities shifted to a negative subsidy position. The general effect of the NFR has been to confirm these differences. Average subsidy per dwelling across England fell by £24.00 in cash terms, equivalent to £55.00 (£1.06 a week) or 38% in real terms. Subsidy has increased in money terms but fallen slightly in real terms in London while increasing slightly in real terms in the metropolitan areas, the northern regions, and in regional centres. Subsidy has declined in non-metropolitan areas, especially in the South. The sharpest subsidy reductions were in the affluent suburbs and rural areas. Before 1990 the typical southern shire district was a zero-subsidy, zero-transfer authority; now it is in significant negative subsidy of the order of £2.00-4.00 per dwelling per week. This is the extent to which the council tenants in these areas could be said to be paying for the rent rebates of their fellow tenants.

Figure 7: Housing element of subsidy, 1987/88 (@ 1991 prices) and 1991/92

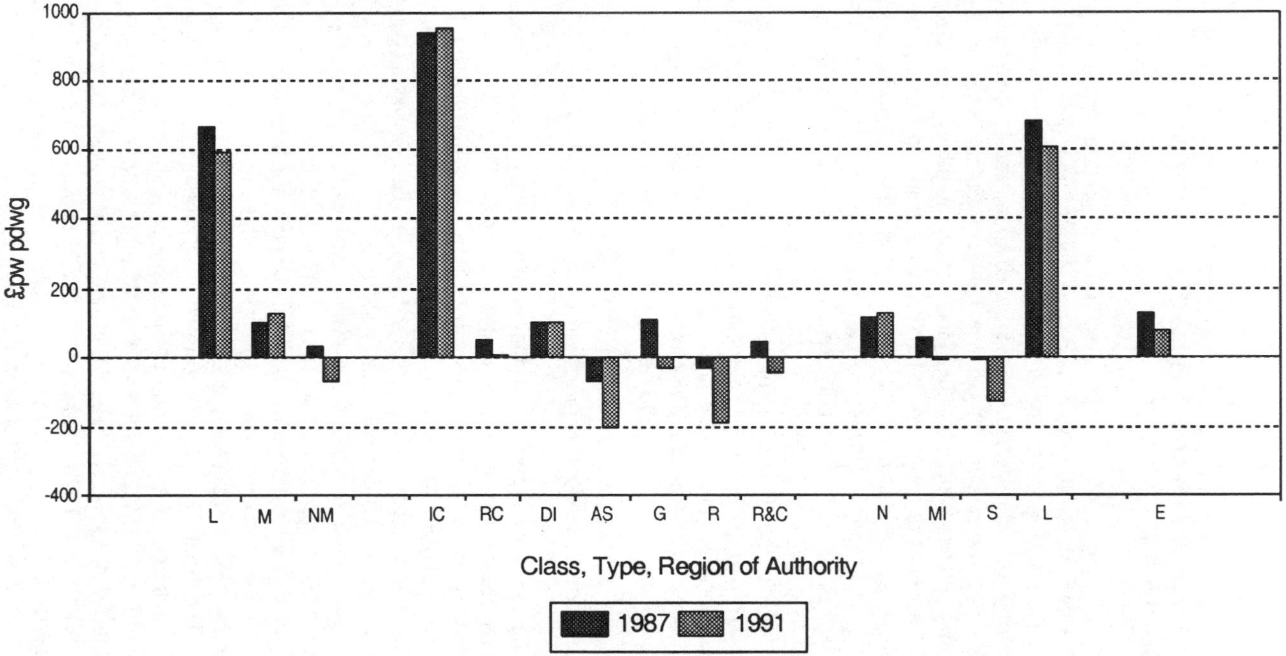

Accounting for changes in HRAs by region and type of area

Data such as that tabulated in Table 3 (in the appendix to this chapter) can be used to provide one kind of way of 'accounting for' outcomes in terms of the key variable of council house rents. The term 'accounting' is used here in its financial sense. In other words, rents correspond to the balance between expenditures on the one hand and subsidies and other incomes on the other, in the HRA. As the account is supposed to balance each year, so changes between one year and another in the 'bottom line' (rents) can be accounted for by changes in all the expenditure and income items. In practice, there is not a precise match because of errors and omissions in the data.

As in the discussion of broad changes above, the two years 1987/88 and 1991/92 are compared, in order to show the impact of transition to the new system and its first two years of operation. Two types of area classifications are commented on: broad regions and types of district based on the Shaw classification.

Changes by broad region

The northern regions had the lowest level of rent increases as intended by the market related guidelines. There were moderate increases in net debt charges and RCCOs. Revenue expenditure on both management and maintenance increased by less than average. The North made a modest gain in subsidy, but this was less than the increase in their debt charges.

The midland regions are rather intermediate in most of their characteristics. Rent rises were rather higher than in the North. Debt charges were static and RCCOs have not been used so much. Both management and maintenance expenditure increased a bit more. The Midlands experienced a modest loss of subsidy.

The South saw significantly higher rent increases. Both debt charges and RCCOs made a modest contribution to this outcome, while the increases in both management and maintenance were significantly higher. The South experienced a substantial loss of subsidy, but it should be noted that this was equivalent to only about 20% of the total cash increase in rents. Two-thirds of the increase was due to management and maintenance.

London saw the largest rent rise. There were large increases in debt charges and RCCOs, quite a large rise in repair and maintenance and a very large rise indeed in supervision and management. Extra provision had to be made for working balances, and there was a very large rise in "other expenditure minus other income", accounting for 15% of the rent rise. It is not clear exactly what this comprises, but it probably includes private sector leasing costs, provision for arrears, loss of contributions in respect of transferred stock, deferred purchase and other items. London gained subsidy, but this increase was only half of the increase in net debt charges. In general, London gives an impression of a transition to the new regime in which not all of the special costs particularly associated with London were picked up.

It is worth noting that net debt charges did not fall in most areas. The reason must be that debt charge figures in Table 3 are for net debt charges (see appendix, p 66). Many authorities were earning substantial interest income on unspent receipts in the late 1980s, removed since from the HRA. Interest rates are also higher while the level of council house sales has fallen sharply. Both repair and maintenance (revenue) and supervision and management rose in real terms in most areas. This was, in accounting terms, the main factor underlying the rise in rents. Other incomes did not rise much and in London were swamped by other expenditures. Working balances were less available in general and many authorities started to use RCCOs. These other factors were of some importance, alongside subsidy change, in accounting for changes in rents.

Changes by type of area

- Inner-city authorities include many inner London boroughs and so the pattern is similar to the London one described above. Inner cities had the highest rent rises and large increases in most types of expenditure, particularly debt charges. Their spending, however, on repairs and maintenance increased less than on supervision and management. These areas had a large gain in subsidy.

- Regional centres had moderate rent rises and most components of change were moderate. Supervision and management showed a low increase.

- Declining industrial areas had the lowest increases in rent and expenditure. They made a modest gain in subsidy matched by a similar rise in debt charges.

- Affluent suburbs contrast strongly; they had a high rent rise to finance a large increase in RCCOs and repair and maintenance programmes, and to offset a large loss in subsidy.

- Growth areas had rather average values on many of the changes, including some loss of subsidy.

- Rural districts had average rent rises. Their debt charges and RCCOs increased, but their M&M expenditure showed an average level of increase. Rural districts experienced a large subsidy loss.

- Resort and coastal districts were a more moderate version of the affluent suburbs. Their rents rose above the average. Debt charges and RCCOs increased as did supervision and management. These areas experienced a moderate loss of subsidy.

Statistical analysis of local responses

The last part of this chapter seeks to generalise about and untangle some of the systematic influences on local authority decisions and responses. The comments made are based on the use of regression analysis, the standard statistical technique used to 'explain' variations in particular factors in terms of a number of other factors. More details and the tables of results (Tables 4 and 5) are included in the appendix to this chapter (see pp 68-71).

The two variables which the regression is used to explain are the change in rents and the change in spending on management and maintenance per dwelling between 1987/88 and 1991/92. These are the main elements which are left to the councils to decide for themselves each year. Although the NFR tends to link these two variables together, as explained in Chapter 2, there are enough other factors at work tending to 'de-couple' rents and spending that it is worthwhile looking at the two separately.

Explaining rent changes

We know that rents have risen everywhere, but much more in some areas than others (see Figure 1). How much of this variation is due to the direct intentions of the government, expressed through the parameters of the NFR, and how much to other local contingencies or local political choices?

The first conclusion is that quite a large part of the variation (more than half) cannot be explained simply and systematically by the data assembled. This could be taken as evidence that local autonomy is alive and well in the field of council housing, despite the NFR. However, unexplained variance could also be due to a number of other factors: these include the need to make provision for rent arrears, subsidy withdrawal where voids were above the government's allowance, creative accounting coming home to roost (eg deferred purchase), and short-term leasing. Systematic data on these factors was not readily available for this analysis. Finally unexplained variance can also reflect errors in the data or omissions of other important factors.

The second conclusion is that the basic parameters of the subsidy regime - rent guideline, M&M allowance, and/or subsidy leverage (subsidy changes adjusted for debt charges) - do not explain a lot of the variance. It is necessary to introduce a number of other factors - local circumstances, financial factors, and choice/preference factors - to get a more reasonable explanation. Insofar as these local contingencies are outside the control of local authorities and reasonable, their significance could be taken to indicate that the NFR is not a wholly adequate instrument for the recognition of local circumstances.

A key question, for our understanding of implementation, is whether the guidelines have more or less potent effects than the cash subsidy amounts. Are local authorities guideline-followers or basically economic agents chiefly influenced by cash? The evidence is not completely clear, but it tends towards the view that both guidelines and cash are important. Simple models without the extra variables give a much better fit when the guidelines are used than when the subsidy leverage variable is used. The results indicate that rent guidelines are matched to the extent of 79p in £1.00 whereas subsidy change is only matched to about 30p in £1.00 (translating from weekly to yearly). Both these figures fall in the more complex models, to 32-44p and 19p respectively. On the other hand, when other variables are included, the model including subsidy leverage fits better than the model using only guidelines, while the model with both is no better than the subsidy model. There is also evidence that subsidy withdrawal has a stronger effect on rents (73p in £1.00) than subsidy increases, and that a model that recognises this works better still. Thus, overall the evidence on this interesting implementation question is rather mixed.

A simple view of the NFR is that rents should be expected to follow rent guidelines, but not to be influenced by M&M allowances. As has been shown, rents do follow guidelines quite strongly, but what about allowances? Allowances could affect rents negatively, at least in models excluding the subsidy variable, because of the cash subsidy effect. Alternatively, allowances might act as need proxies and show a positive relationship with expenditure change. With the introduction of targeting, allowances are partially related to needs, but damping means that differences are not fully reflected in the allowances. If authorities with high needs and relatively high allowances actually increased spending significantly more than average, they would be forced to raise rents and there would be a positive correlation between allowances and rent increases. The results suggest a weak positive relationship not always statistically significant. In other words, the need proxy effect is stronger than the cash subsidy effect. This indication that locally perceived needs vary more than present damped M&M allowances is interesting but unsurprising.

The result that rents are affected more by subsidy withdrawal than by subsidy increase is in line with a prior hypothesis, as follows. Local authorities have little political incentive to reduce rents, but are willing to increase them where necessary, especially where central government's withdrawal of subsidy can be blamed. Authorities are anxious to protect their existing levels of M&M expenditure (ie existing service levels and staffing); they would like to increase it where financially possible, particularly if the government seems to be paying. The consequence of these motivational assumptions is that the relationship between subsidy change and rents alters when one moves from subsidy withdrawal to subsidy increase. There is a stronger negative effect on rents where subsidy change is negative (73p in £1.00).

Certain factors representing the financial position of authorities in the late 1980s were tested in the models. These only seem to have a slight effect, with one exception. Change in stock probably mainly reflects the rate of right to buy sales in the late 1980s. Authorities which sold more of their stock enjoyed a more favourable local financial environment and seemed to be able to carry some financial benefit forward into the NFR in the form of lower rent rises.

A number of need and cost factors were tested. One of these is a cost index which has a strong effect although one which varies from model to model. Another is the estimate of backlog disrepair in the council stock which shows no relationship with rent increases. The recent history of capitalised repairs in the period 1987/89 seems to play a more significant role. Local authorities with a lot of capitalised repairs, which they could not continue with after 1990, have tended to increase their rents more. In general they would have done this in order to substitute revenue and RCCO funded work although, as Figures 3 and 4 show, the extent of substitution is low (see pp 45-46). Size of stock was included to test whether large housing authorities increase their rents more or less than small ones. In general, larger council stocks are associated with higher rent rises, between 4p and 7p per week per thousand dwellings. This might indirectly reflect diseconomies of scale, or differences in the difficulty of the management task, but could equally reflect different service standards, or political choices.

The possible effects of rebates on rents policies (and the related expenditure policies) are of interest. One hypothesis is that local authorities now realise that all those tenants on housing benefit pay zero marginal contribution to rent increases, since the 1988 housing benefit reform, and that they, therefore, tend to choose high-spend (high service), high-rent policies, especially where most tenants are on housing benefit. An alternative, contradictory hypothesis is the affordability one, namely that housing benefit dependence is an indicator of poverty and affordability problems and also that it is highly undesirable because of its poverty trap effects. Since higher rents raise the housing benefit dependence, this could lead to local authorities with higher dependence being more loath to increase rents. The results are more consistent with the first hypothesis than with the second, although for technical reasons this should be interpreted with caution.

Last but not least, the influence of local politics should be considered. Students of politics will be glad to learn that the evidence suggests that 'politics do matter' still, in this instance. The evidence is that Conservative councils increased rents more, by nearly £2.00 per week over this period, other things being equal. The Labour effect is less clear statistically, but it suggests a tendency to set lower rent rises, relative to councils with other or no overall control.

Explaining changes in M&M expenditure

Table 5 in the appendix shows the effects of applying the same sets of explanatory variables to M&M expenditure changes between 1987/88 and 1991/92 (see pp 70-71).

As with rents, only a minority of variance in this policy output can be explained using systematic factors. Very little can be explained by subsidy leverage or the NFR guidelines/allowances on their own. The explanation is better when other variables, including need and cost factors and financial and political factors are included. Management and maintenance may be inherently more subject to other influences than rents. But it is also relevant that, prior to 1992, the M&M allowance changes did not vary very much for most local authorities due to slow progress with targeting and damping. Therefore, it would be surprising if this factor did explain much. In the full models the effect of allowance changes is quite large and significant (up to 76p in £1.00). This may be due to its role as a proxy for need, or an indicator of expected future change in allowance.

The effect of subsidy leverage on M&M expenditure is weak in all models and not statistically significant in several cases. Only where positive and negative subsidy changes are split, for the reasons discussed above, does one begin to see sizeable (43p per £1.00) and significant effects of subsidy on spending in the case of subsidy increases.

A simple view of the NFR is that management and maintenance should tend to follow the allowance and not be affected by the rent guidelines (which affect rents). In practice, rent guidelines seem to have a negative effect when included at a rate of up to 25p in £1.00; the fact that this drops to an insignificant level when subsidy is also included indicates that this effect works through cash subsidy. This illustrates the problem of the NFR as a system pursuing at least two objectives using only one hard instrument (subsidy).

Some financial factors relating to the situation of authorities in the late 1980s were included. Having no subsidy in 1987/88 meant a softer regime, and this could have resulted in higher expenditure in that period. If that expenditure had dealt with more of the problems, such local authorities could manage with a smaller increase in expenditure under the new regime. The negative effects of this variable in some models support this hypothesis. Having higher working balances in 1987 is associated with higher expenditure increases. Authorities whose stock declined less tended to have larger expenditure increases, probably because of right to buy sales benefits.

Some need and cost factors are significant. The cost index should be positive because, simply to maintain service standards, local authorities in high cost areas must increase spending by a larger absolute amount per dwelling. This is reflected in most of the models. Local authorities with a larger council stock increased their spending rather more, but this is not always statistically significant. Mention has already been made of the role of M&M allowances as a needs measure for recurrent spending and this does have some positive association with expenditure. However, the measure of disrepair backlog is not significant in any model. This result rather confirms the point already made about targeting: that there is no correlation between this index and the level of repair and maintenance spending in either 1987/88 or 1991/92. This may indicate that expenditure changes do not respond to or reflect need in any degree. Alternatively, it may indicate that this index is deficient and/or that need is picked up elsewhere.

Capitalised repairs were very important in 1987/88, as important as revenue expenditure in some areas (Figure 3). The ability to fund repairs in this way has now been sharply curtailed. Some tendency to substitute revenue spending in areas where previously capitalised repairs were high may be expected. This assumes those programmes reflected high needs and did not in themselves wipe out those needs, and that local authorities wished to see those programmes continue in some measure. In two of the models the expected positive relationship is observed; in the other two the relationship is negative but not statistically significant. This instability reflects intercorrelations with other variables.

Finally, what were the political party influences on expenditure? Conservative councils not only increased rents more, but they appeared to spend them on management and maintenance. The Labour effect is a smaller, less significant negative one. While the finding that Conservative councils set higher rents is unsurprising, the corollary, that they spend more on services for their tenants, may seem slightly surprising or paradoxical to some. It is another way of making the point, shown graphically on Figures 4-6, that some of the highest expenditures on management and maintenance are in the affluent suburbs and resort/coastal districts of the South.

Conclusions

The government has achieved its goal of seeing rents rise in real terms, particularly in London and the South, so that rents now show a pattern quite similar to market values. Rents tend to be above guideline levels in most areas, mainly because M&M expenditure exceeds allowances substantially.

There has been a striking fall in the volume of repair and maintenance activity in all areas, particularly in London and other cities where problems of disrepair tend to be worse. This fall is due to the new capital control system and the much-reduced availability of capital receipts. It has only been offset to a small extent by higher spending financed directly from rents.

As Chapter 3 showed, some progress has been made in developing targeted allowances for the distribution of subsidy. But, looking at actual patterns of expenditure, including capitalised repairs, the goal of targeting spending to areas of greater need has not been achieved so far; in some respects spending is less well targeted than before.

There has been a real rise in housing management expenditure. While the reasons for this are understandable, the shifting balance between management and repair/maintenance expenditure is perhaps questionable.   M&M spending exceeds allowance significantly and this applies in all types of area. Both expenditure and allowances reflect past spending patterns which were influenced by resource availability.

As in the 1980s system, subsidy is concentrated in London with a slight shift to some northern urban areas. The transition appears to have failed to cover all of the special costs arising in London, despite the concentration of subsidy. Detailed examples of this are discussed in the next chapter. The typical southern shire district has lost subsidy and now has a significant negative subsidy entitlement.

The largest factor accounting for the general rise in rents is the rise in revenue spending on M&M. The loss of subsidy is less significant in cash terms, but quite important in the South.

The situations of individual local authorities are very variable. Subsidy and guideline changes do not translate simply into equivalent outcomes and they do not statistically predict a high proportion of the actual changes in rents and spending. This is partly a reflection of the continuing strong exercise of local discretion and partly due to errors and omissions in either the system or the data. The ways that particular local circumstances cause outcomes to deviate from guidelines are illustrated in the next chapter.

Local authorities seem to be influenced by both guidelines and their cash subsidy position. Subsidy withdrawal tends to lead to higher rents while extra subsidy tends to lead to higher expenditure.

A number of other influences on rents and expenditure can be identified statistically. Some need and cost indicators are significant, but backlog repairs do not seem to be related to spending increases. Some of the benefits of more favourable financial situations facing some authorities before 1990 seem to carry through into the new system. Varying local policy preferences clearly also play a part, as becomes clearer in the next chapter. Conservative councils tend to have followed policies of higher rent increases with higher spending.

APPENDIX

This appendix contains three tables of more detailed statistical results together with some explanatory technical notes. Table 3 provides a detailed account of the changes in expenditure, income and rents by region and type of authority between 1987/88 and 1991/92 referred to earlier in this chapter. Tables 4 and 5 provide the results of the regression models used to 'explain' variations in rent and expenditure changes, as discussed in the last part of the chapter.

The financial data are derived principally from three sources: first, CIPFA Statistical Information Service, which compiles data annually on local authority HRA expenditure and income and housing rents; second, the DOE, which kindly supplied a full set of data from the housing subsidy claim form for 1991/92 (second advanced claim); and third, the annual ADC/AMA Housing Finance Survey for 1992, the data for which was analysed at SAUS. A number of other indicators are used in the analysis, derived mainly from the existing SAUS housing database, but supplemented in a few cases by additional data, for example from the DOE based on local authority HIP returns.

The analysis concentrates on a few key variables which describe the main dimensions of impact of the new system. These are rents, expenditure on repair and maintenance and on supervision and management, and housing subsidy. These variables are normally expressed as amounts in pounds per dwelling per year (or per week in the case of rents). Most tables and graphs are based on average values for these per dwelling amounts weighted by the local authority housing stock; this means that the results are a true measure of the average value for council tenants. It should be remembered that different tables using different data sources are subject to varying numbers of missing cases; for example, the maximum response to the 1992 ADC/AMA survey was 282. The first 18 authorities to exercise the large scale voluntary transfer (LSVT) of stock to a housing association in this period are excluded from the analysis.

Both the graphs and Table 3 use a simplified version of the Shaw classification of local authorities. This particular classification is based mainly on 1981 Census data and was undertaken by Mark Shaw for the Audit Commission. The idea is to group authorities into clusters or 'families' which have similar characteristics. The technique was originally associated with the work of Webber and Craig (1978). The Shaw classification breaks authorities into 31 groups which are collapsed into the 7 groups used here. A list of individual authorities showing their Shaw category is included in Appendix 3 of Bramley (1991).

Under the new financial regime the local authority has two main decisions to make: the level of rents and the level of M&M expenditure. These two decisions are now (since 1990) closely connected by a budget constraint set by the new financial regime; given an amount of subsidy, £1.00 more on M&M expenditure requires £1.00 more on rents. Prior to 1990 this was less clear cut and depended on the subsidy status and other factors. Even now the two decisions are slightly de-coupled by such factors as balances, RCCOs, other incomes and unsubsidised expenditures. In fitting regression models to explain decisions on these two key policy outputs, expenditure and rents, the interaction of these two elements, namely the budget constraint set by the regime and the exercise of local policy discretion, is being remodelled. In exploratory work like this, and because of the partial de-coupling and change of regime, it is justified to fit regression models separately to the two variables (rents and M&M) rather than to a single variable or some more complex model.

Since our dependent variables are in cash it is desirable to include a cost index. The DOE's cost index used for adjusting the government generalised needs index (GNI), under which London costs are 40% above the North (i.e. the variable takes values between 1.0 and 1.4, and the London-North difference is estimated as 40% of the coefficient) is used for this purpose. This variable is usually positive and significant, but less so in the models with guidelines/allowances because these variables are strongly correlated. It is possible that the effects of this variable are exaggerated by its acting as a proxy for other London effects, some of which might be to do with local policies. An alternative procedure might be to deflate the dependent variables prior to undertaking the regressions.

Backlog repairs are based on two numbers, the local authorities' own estimates (on the HIP1 form) of council dwellings in disrepair or unfit, and the DOE's needs (GNI) indicator for local authority stock condition. It does not seem to have any significant influence in either equation. In the rents equation this could indicate that the NFR is successful in compensating for needs variations, a slightly implausible hypothesis given the state of targeting methodology.

The proportion of rent rebates seems to have a positive effect, particularly in the rent change models. However, before drawing strong policy conclusions it should be remembered that the causality may run the other way: ie this may be picking up the mechanical takeup relationship between rent level and housing benefit takeup, not the behavioural element of rent determination. A more standardised measure of housing benefit potential takeup is needed to overcome this problem.

Table 3: Breakdown of HRA income and expenditure changes 1987/88 to 1991/92 (£ per dwelling per year)

	Rent Change 1987-91	Debt Charges 1987-91	RCCO Change 1987-91	R&M Change 1987-91	S&M Change 1987-91	Other Exp-Inc 1987-91	Working Balances 1987-91	Subsidy Change 1987-91
Class of authority:								
London	821.6	162.2	29.6	214.1	301.0	126.8	35.8	82.3
Metropolitan	350.4	90.5	30.2	196.1	103.2	4.8	-37.6	45.7
Non-Metropolitan	487.0	23.0	35.1	176.2	152.7	-13.2	-21.6	-91.5
Broad type of district:								
Inner city	741.1	282.1	30.7	159.4	292.2	115.0	56.9	232.1
Regional centre	465.9	61.8	29.1	206.7	133.8	-11.1	-32.9	-34.9
Declining industry	312.6	61.9	31.8	167.2	103.6	6.4	-31.7	29.4
Affluent suburb	645.3	-1.2	47.4	254.2	194.1	-4.6	-34.1	-148.3
Growing	500.7	28.9	12.6	166.9	154.8	0.3	-18.5	-118.4
Rural	501.0	-74.6	43.6	176.7	147.7	-17.9	-15.4	-168.5
Resort/coastal	591.7	95.1	41.1	159.4	178.1	6.2	-10.2	-76.0
Broad region:								
North	325.0	86.0	40.9	164.9	104.6	-0.8	-32.0	41.1
Midlands	419.6	8.2	16.9	191.1	138.1	-10.0	-34.7	-52.8
South	586.4	39.3	37.8	202.4	166.1	-9.6	-16.5	-126.3
London	821.3	160.0	28.2	220.2	298.8	126.0	34.8	81.3
England	**477.1**	**61.9**	**32.6**	**188.1**	**151.9**	**8.7**	**-20.8**	**-24.3**

Table 4: Regression models to explain change in rents 1987-1991 (£ per dwelling per week)

Explanatory variables	(1)	(2)	(3)	(4)	(5)	(6)
Constant	9.37 (26.3)	0.41 (0.3)	-9.98 (-2.5)	-4.79 (-1.1)	-10.46 (-3.0)	-2.25 (-0.5)
Subsidy leverage	-0.0057 (-3.5)***		-0.0036 (-2.3)**			-0.0063 (-3.6)***
Positive subsidy leverage		0.0021 (0.9)			0.0090 (3.6)***	
Negative subsidy leverage		-0.148 (-6.1)***			-0.014 (-6.3)***	
Rent guideline increase		0.377 (4.3)***		0.439 (3.6)***		0.320 (2.4)**
M&M allowance increase		0.0062 (2.8)		0.0045 (1.3)		0.0072 (2.0)**
No subsidy 1987			-0.0039 (-1.3)	-0.0009 (-0.3)	0.00047 (0.2)	-0.0046 (-1.3)
Working balance 1987			0.0014 (0.6)	0.0023 (0.9)	0.0017 (0.8)	0.0011 (0.4)
Cost index (ratio to North)			14.00 (5.1)***	3.00 (0.8)	12.5 (5.1)***	1.38 (0.4)
Estimated disrepair			0.000012 (0.1)	-0.000007 (-0.7)	0.000005 (0.1)	0.00004 (0.4)

Explanatory variables	(1)	(2)	(3)	(4)	(5)	(6)
Capitalised repairs 1987-89			0.0017 (2.1)**	0.00013 (0.1)	0.0016 (2.25)**	-0.00015 (-0.1)
Stock 1987 (000)			0.05 (1.6)	0.04 (1.2)	0.07 (2.4)**	0.038 (1.2)
Stock change			0.54 (2.1)**	0.45 (1.7)*	0.63 (2.7)***	0.46 (1.8)*
Rebates proportion (%)			0.053 (1.3)	0.090 (2.3)**	0.066 (2.0)**	0.073 (1.7)*
Conservative control			1.97 (2.7)***	1.82 (2.4)***	1.79 (2.8)***	2.01 (2.5)**
Labour control			-0.72 (-1.1)	-0.37 (-0.5)	-0.86 (-1.4)	0.13 (0.2)
Adj r-squared	0.044	0.350	0.327	0.271	0.409	0.319
F ratio	11.9	29.0	10.8	7.1	15.4	7.2
N	250	208	222	197	250	172

Notes:
1. Most financial variables are expressed in £ per dwelling per year, except rents which are per week.
2. 'No subsidy' and political control variables are dummy variables taking the values 0 (no) or 1 (yes).
3. Figures in brackets are t-statistics; asterisks denote significance at 10%/5%/1% levels.
4. Subsidy includes RFCs and rate/general fund transfers (negative), and 'housing element' in 1991/92.
5. 'Subsidy leverage' is the subsidy change minus net debt charge change.
6. All equations are weighted by stock and have three outliers removed.
7. Numbers of cases vary due to missing data.

Table 5: Regression models to explain change in M&M expenditure 1987-91 (£ per dwelling per year)

Explanatory variables	(1)	(2)	(3)	(4)	(5)	(6)
Constant	359.6 ()	-4.6 (-0.1)	-446 (-3.0)	336 (2.3)	-236 (-1.7)	104 (0.6)
Subsidy leverage	0.084 (1.4)		0.122 (2.2)**			-0.009 (-0.1)
Positive subsidy leverage		0.190 (2.2)**			0.427 (4.3)***	
Negative subsidy leverage		-0.173 (-1.9)*			-0.033 (-0.4)	
Rent guideline increase		0.92 (0.3)		-12.8 (-2.9)***		-4.30 (-0.9)
M&M allowance increase		0.638 (7.7)***		0.694 (4.4)***		0.761 (5.9)***
No subsidy 1987			-0.335 (-3.2)***	-0.324 (-2.8)***	-0.045 (-0.4)	-0.063 (-0.9)
Working balance 1987			0.127 (1.5)	-0.016 (-0.2)	0.162 (1.9)*	0.191 (1.9)*
Cost index (ratio to North)			491 (4.9)***	-253 (-2.2)**	432 (4.4)***	58 (0.4)
Estimated disrepair backlog			1704 (0.4)	-294 (-0.1)	2469 (0.8)	0.00055 (0.1)

Explanatory variables	(1)	(2)	(3)	(4)	(5)	(6)
Capitalised repairs 1987-89			0.144 (4.1)***	-0.03 (-0.7)	0.085 (3.0)***	-0.059 (-1.4)
Stock 1987 (000)			0.16 (0.1)	5.0 (4.4)***	2.0 (1.9)*	1.29 (1.1)
Stock change			-2.9 (0.3)	28 (3.0)**	10.4 (1.1)	5.9 (0.6)
Rebates proportion (%)			3.69 (2.5)*	-1.98 (-1.5)	-0.074 (-0.1)	-0.04 (-0.0)
Conservative control			39.2 (1.4)	19.6 (0.8)	61.8 (2.4)**	77.2 (2.7)***
Labour control			-44.6 (-1.7)*	-24 (-1.0)	-7.0 (-0.3)	-0.59 (-0.0)
Adj r-squared	0.0044	0.310	0.338	0.320	0.283	0.317
F ratio	2.1	24.3	11.3	8.7	9.2	7.2
N	350?	208	222	197	250	172

Notes:

1. Most financial variables are expressed in £ per dwelling per year, except rents which are per week.
2. 'No subsidy' and political control variables are dummy variables taking the values 0 (no) or 1 (yes).
3. Figures in brackets are t-statistics; asterisks denote significance at 10%/5%/1% levels.
4. Subsidy includes RFCs and rate/general fund transfers (negative), and 'housing element' in 1991/92.
5. 'Subsidy leverage' is the subsidy change minus net debt charge change.
6. All equations are weighted by stock and have three outliers removed.
7. Numbers of cases vary due to missing data.

five

POLICY AND PRACTICE AT THE LOCAL LEVEL

Introduction

The previous chapter looked at the implementation of the NFR in terms of the emerging national and regional pattern of outcomes. This chapter moves the focus to the local level and draws on a series of case studies carried out in a total of 15 local authorities in 1990/91 and 1991/92. The material presented here draws on a large amount of documentary evidence provided by the authorities and interviews with the key actors in the various authorities. In most cases meetings were held with the director of housing, the chair of housing and other relevant staff in the housing and treasurer's departments.

Work at the level of the individual local authority provides a valuable complement to the more aggregated analysis of the previous chapter, giving both a sub-regional perspective on the impact of policy and an insight into local implementation processes.

At the aggregate level it is clear that rents and M&M spending have both risen by more than the assumptions built into the subsidy system. Nevertheless the government has been able to make some progress towards its objectives of (i) a pattern of rents which more accurately reflects differences in property values across the country, and (ii) greater control over the level and distribution of subsidy. The purpose of the case studies was to get beneath the aggregated data and to investigate the local implications of, and responses to, the NFR: to explore with local authorities how they were affected by the new system and how they had decided on their particular local policies in the light of the legislation. The key questions here concern the extent to which local decisions were produced by the constraints of the system or by the exercise of local discretion.

The starting point is the observation that local authorities entered the NFR from different directions and in different circumstances, in terms of their local housing problems, their financial position and their politics and policies. The system brought with it very different implications and degrees of constraint for different authorities, and the authorities themselves have produced a wide range of responses. This emphasis on variation reflects the structure of British government and the fact that local housing authorities have a history of considerable autonomy from central government. Over many years the continued exercise of local policy-making powers tends to accentuate differences among authorities. In order to understand the implementation of central government housing policy, therefore, it is necessary to take into account not only the extent to which housing problems vary from place to place but also the policy-making role of local authorities themselves. The NFR is designed to give local authorities a degree of freedom to make their own policy decisions.

In a sense central policy is just one set of factors to be considered in the formulation of local policy. Local authorities receive central government policy and then they digest, interpret and take it into account in the production of their own policy outputs, which in turn lead to local policy outcomes. Local authorities are clearly important in the implementation of central government policy, but they do not always share the objectives of that policy nor define their responsibility in terms of achieving those objectives. This perspective was expressed with some force by the chair of housing in one of the northern case study authorities. His argument was that he had been elected to do a particular job which was quite different from the one that the government had been elected to do; he therefore saw the rent guideline as irrelevant, except that it generated problems to be managed.

The authorities

Local housing authorities in England and Wales are highly diverse in character, reflecting differences in location and economic activity as well as population, size and density. The largest municipal landlords, such as Birmingham, Leeds and Sheffield, still retain stocks of more than 70,000 dwellings, whereas the smallest, including Eden, Teesdale and Epsom and Ewell, have under 2,000. A growing number of authorities, of course, have transferred their properties to new housing associations and, therefore, have no stock at all. The case study authorities discussed in this chapter were selected to reflect the diversity across the country, in terms of geographical spread, differences in stock size and type of authority (London, metropolitan and shire districts). They are not, however, a 'typical' set of authorities; on the contrary, several were selected because they were particularly interesting in the context of research on the NFR. Table 6 lists the 15 authorities and gives some basic information about population and housing stock.

In terms of property values as revealed through right to buy valuations, the case study authorities include those virtually at the top and bottom of the range. Only Kensington and Chelsea has higher recorded values than Hammersmith and Fulham, and at the other end of the spectrum, Derwentside is in the bottom ten. In terms of rents, too, the authorities illustrate the range of rents charged in the year before the NFR was introduced. Hammersmith and Fulham and Torbay were in the top ten, while Exeter had the lowest average rent in England.

Tables 7 and 8 show the guideline and actual increases in the case study authorities in the first three years of the NFR. Thirteen of the authorities have increased rents by more than the guideline, although the extent to which they have done so varies from under 1% in Exeter to almost 45% in Hackney. As previous chapters have pointed out, an important factor in the steeper rise in actual rents has been that expenditure on management and maintenance has exceeded allowances, and this is the case in 12 of the case study authorities, as Table 9 shows.

Table 10 shows how the guideline rents and M&M allowances implied quite different levels of leverage on rents in the whole group of case study authorities in the first three years of the NFR. The amount of leverage is indicated in the final column, (a) - (b).

Table 6:   The case study authorities, listed by property value

	Population 1981	Average housing stock 1991/92	Average rent 1989/90	Average right to buy value 1987/88 to 1990/91 Houses (£)	Flats (£)
Hammersmith/Fulham	148,100	18,502	29.34	77,454	58,174
Hackney	180,200	45,123	20.17	66,129	45,440
Barking/Dagenham	150,200	26,336	16.16	58,105	49,791
Cotswold	68,400	4,852	21.94	49,645	42,457
St Edmundsbury	86,100	7,856	16.38	45,176	38,113
Exeter	96,100	6,750	14.71	43,491	36,817
Torbay	115,600	3,278	29.31	38,916	34,768
Leicester	279,800	29,893	24.10	28,924	21,620
Cardiff	287,000	18,220	24.11	28,606	
Sandwell	307,400	47,760	22.29	25,905	17,792
Knowsley	173,400	22,675	23.86	21,590	12,087
Rhymney Valley		9,413	25.0	21,099	
N Tyneside	198,000	24,923	16.31	21,009	14,454
Middlesbrough	149,800	15,852	27.75	18,297	14,546
Derwentside	88,100	11,058	19.94	17,570	14,546

Sources: Census 1981, the authorities and DOE

Table 7: Guideline rent increases, 1990/91 to 1992/93

	Rent level 1989 £ pw	Rent increases 1990/91 £ pw	Rent increases 1991/92 £ pw	Rent increases 1992/92 £ pw	Total increase 1989-93 £ pw	Total increase 1989-93 %
Hammersmith/Fulham	33.32	1.70	2.50	4.05	8.25	24.7
Hackney	20.17	4.50	2.50	4.41	11.41	56.6
Barking/Dagenham	16.16	4.50	2.50	4.50	11.50	71.2
Cotswold	21.94	4.44	2.50	4.32	11.25	51.3
St Edmundsbury	16.38	3.45	2.50	4.50	10.45	63.8
Exeter	14.71	4.50	2.50	4.31	11.31	76.9
Torbay	29.31	0.95	1.38	1.20	3.53	12.0
Leicester	24.10	0.95	1.38	1.20	3.53	14.6
Cardiff	24.11	1.32	2.07	2.66	6.05	25.1
Sandwell	22.29	0.95	1.38	1.20	3.53	15.8
Knowsley	23.86	0.95	1.38	1.20	3.53	14.8
Rhymney Valley	25.06	1.35	1.50	1.13	3.98	15.9
N Tyneside	16.31	0.95	1.38	1.20	3.53	21.4
Middlesbrough	27.75	0.95	1.38	1.20	3.53	12.7
Derwentside	19.94	0.95	1.38	1.20	3.53	17.7

Sources: Census 1981, the authorities and DOE

Table 8: Actual rent increases, 1990/91 to 1992/93

	Rent level 1989 £ pw	Rent increases 1990/91 £ pw	Rent increases 1991/92 £ pw	Rent increases 1992/92 £ pw	Total increase 1989-93 £ pw	Total increase 1989-93 %
Hammersmith/Fulham	29.34	3.98	5.95	1.95	11.88	40.5
Hackney	20.17	5.23	6.33	8.89	20.45	101.4
Barking/Dagenham	16.16	2.70	3.50	3.00	9.20	56.9
Cotswold	21.94	9.00	5.00	4.32	18.32	83.5
St Edmundsbury	16.38	4.00	3.00	3.98	10.98	67.0
Exeter	14.71	4.60	2.50	4.31	11.41	77.6
Torbay	29.31	4.39	3.37	1.80	9.56	32.6
Leicester	24.10	1.64	2.10	2.38	6.12	25.4
Cardiff	24.11	1.99	1.98	2.90	6.87	28.1
Sandwell	22.29	4.62	2.90	2.30	9.82	44.0
Knowsley	23.86	1.52	3.93	2.50	7.95	33.3
Rhymney Valley	25.06	3.32	1.85	3.00	8.17	32.6
N Tyneside	16.31	3.00	1.36	1.02	3.16	19.4
Middlesbrough	27.75	0.95	1.20	2.50	4.65	16.7
Derwentside	19.94	6.28	1.29	2.08	9.65	48.4

Sources: Census 1981, the authorities and DOE

Table 9:   Management and maintenance allowances and actuals

	1990/91		1991/92		1992/93	
	All.	Act.	All.	Act.	All.	Act.
Hammersmith/Fulham	1275	1393	1402	1594	1486	-
Hackney	1102	1539	1199	1196	1331	-
Barking/Dagenham	685	660	748	762	1055	-
Cotswold	991	1034	991	1044	1026	-
St Edmundsbury	569	667	600	744	634	-
Exeter	655	788	691	748	746	-
Torbay	559	739	590	788	664	-
Leicester	722	738	762	857	789	-
Cardiff	885	885	885	993	917	-
Sandwell	586	809	618	891	695	-
Knowsley	809	796	853	979	883	-
Rhymney Valley	643	705	772	-	-	-
N Tyneside	508	539	579	611	623	-
Middlesbrough	732	637	773	730	800	-
Derwentside	559	600	590	708	611	-

Sources: Census 1981, the authorities and DOE

Table 10: Changes in guideline rents and M&M allowances 1990/91 to 1992/93 (£ per year)

	Aggregate guideline rent increase (a)	Aggregate M&M allowance increase (b)	(a) - (b)
Hammersmith/Fulham	429	306	123
Hackney	593	311	282
Barking/Dagenham	598	421	177
Cotswold	585	109	476
St Edmundsbury	543	107	436
Exeter	588	142	448
Torbay	183	149	37
Leicester	183	121	62
Cardiff	315	98	217
Sandwell	183	152	31
Knowsley	183	134	49
Rhymney Valley	183	177	6
N Tyneside	183	155	28
Middlesbrough	183	122	61
Derwentside	183	93	90

Source: DOE determinations

The relationship between guideline rent increases and M&M allowances gives some indication of the rate of subsidy withdrawal in different areas, and the final column in Table 10 shows that in Cotswold, for example, the notional rent increase exceeds the increase in M&M allowance by more than £9.00 per week (or £476.00 per year). This clearly amounts to considerable leverage on rents, compared with the situation in Rhymney Valley or North Tyneside. It is worth adding to the reference to Cotswold, since it is not one of the authorities to feature in the main part of this chapter.

Cotswold went into the NFR with an average rent of only 27p below the national average, but it had a recent history of very high levels of revenue-funded repairs expenditure resulting from a policy of using potential HRA surpluses to improve the stock. This policy was, in a sense, the opposite of capitalising repairs and had the opposite effect, ie it enhanced the authority's opening M&M allowance. However, as an authority with high right to buy valuations Cotswold was given very nearly the maximum guideline rent increase over the first three years of the NFR. And because of the nature of its predominantly rural housing stock it was considered to be spending well above target levels on management and maintenance, with the result that it received little increase in allowances. There was a nil increase in 1991/92 and the minimum 3.5% in 1992/93.

Space precludes a detailed account of each of the case study authorities, and the following discussion is in two main parts; the first looks at the annual round of decision making at the local level, using illustrative material from a number of the case study authorities, and the second deals with policy responses, drawing mainly on those authorities which fall into four categories relating rents to values.

The annual round at local level

Chapter 3 looked at the annual cycle of bidding, budgeting, spending and accounting at central government level. The equivalent process at local level generally seems to start a little later, not earlier than July and in some places as late as the latter part of November. There is little scope for firm planning for the next financial year until the draft guideline rents and M&M allowances are published by the DOE and WO in the autumn, but then the pace and pressure increases as Christmas approaches and activity can become frenetic in the new year as authorities have to finalise budgets by the end of February. Another factor is that authorities wishing to implement rent increases from 1 April are required to give four weeks' notice, hence the need to make decisions by the end of February.

The production of draft HRA budgets is generally an incremental activity based on the current year's budget and likely outturn expenditure. To this draft can be added expenditure items representing growth aspirations put forward by housing staff or known to be favoured by members. The implied rent increase can then be calculated by setting the spending total against the income generated by existing rent levels, estimated subsidy and other income in the coming year. Some case study authorities reported that their budget-making processes had involved considerable effort to reduce very large potential rent increases down to levels acceptable to their elected members.

Who is involved in the process? In all the case study authorities financial management lies with the treasurer or director of finance, and it usually falls to the housing accountant to draw up an initial draft for discussion. Although housing department staff are involved there is considerable variation in the degree of their participation in the production of budget decisions. In most cases it is clear that finance and housing staff have good and close working relationships. In North Tyneside the council appointed an accountant to the position of assistant director of housing (finance), specifically to respond to the approach of the NFR. In Cardiff the housing accountant works from the housing department, although remaining on the staff of the finance department. On the other hand, in Rhymney Valley there is no separate housing department as such and the principal public sector housing officer was not involved in rent setting until 1991/92. In Barking and Dagenham, too, it is clear that the treasurer's department controls housing finance and that there is much less involvement of housing staff. Authorities vary in the way that officers present their reports to members putting forward HRA budget proposals; in some places the report comes from the treasurer and in others it is a joint report. The point at which members become involved also varies, but it is clear that there are often informal discussions with key members such as the chair of housing and/or the leader, sometimes as early as the summer. In one authority, Rhymney Valley, the decision on the rent increase is not made by the housing committee but by the full council on the recommendation of the policy and resources committee.

Most of the case study authorities do not consult tenants directly on the proposed rent increase, and some were obviously very surprised to learn that others found it possible and constructive to do so within the timetable. In Hackney, for example, in 1992/93 tenants were consulted by means of a questionnaire and a series of public meetings, and were asked to give a view about possible cuts or growth in repairs spending and the impact on rents. Tenants showed a strong majority preference for a modest increase in rents to pay for certain categories of increased repairs spending. In Leicester the Labour-controlled council has a policy of consulting the city's Federation of Tenants' Associations before the proposed rent increase is put to the housing committee. In the process of making the rent increase decision in 1991, the officers had first put forward a proposal for a 15% increase, but this was reduced to 9% in the paper put to tenants' representatives in early January. The tenants' preference was for an increase below the rate of inflation but without cuts in management and maintenance; the outcome was that the council agreed on 7.9%. In 1992 it again looked initially as if the increase might be 15% and it was made known to the public that officers were working to achieve savings. The political leadership had indicated that the increase should be below 10%, and housing department officials achieved this by cutting back on staffing levels (which meant cutting some long-term vacancies from the establishment) and reducing service development aspirations; the final decision was 8.9%.

In Exeter the budget process involves the housing accountant, the director and assistant director of housing who meet to review the draft budget and possible options. They seek the view of the chair of housing on the political priorities, and gather other relevant information, such as the maintenance proposals from the director of planning and property. When the guideline increase and M&M allowance are published the housing accountant firms up the estimates, and the director and chair of housing, together with input from the leader, produce final proposals to be put to committee. In the run-up to the budget for 1992/93 the work was completed in early December, in good time for a committee decision in January. This was a situation in which the authority could achieve a rent increase in line with the guideline without much difficulty, but other authorities have reported considerable difficulty in achieving a politically acceptable budget.

In one case study authority, the production of the budget for 1991/92 began in the late summer but concluded with frantic last minute juggling of figures to satisfy the political leadership. In this authority an HRA working party, chaired by an assistant director of housing and consisting of officers from housing and finance, met during the autumn and produced plans by Christmas. Councillors were consulted in early January; initially contact was with an informal group of leading councillors, followed by the Labour Group and then the housing committee. The working party produced a paper for the Labour Group meeting on 1 February, but on the day of the meeting the director of housing was instructed to produce new figures which were more acceptable to members, and he and the chief executive and director of finance had an emergency meeting to produce another paper. However, the papers for the housing committee meeting on 6 February had already been distributed and so the director of housing had to table amendments at that meeting.

Internal political struggles were more evident in some authorities than others. In one authority the cohesiveness of the political leadership was revealed by the chair of housing who explained that there existed a 'kitchen cabinet' consisting of four of five councillors who often met on Saturday mornings or lunchtimes before going on to watch the local football team in action. Less comradely was the action of the director of finance in a different authority; in the early part of 1992 he put out a paper to members setting out his view of the necessary rent increase, without consultation with the director of housing, who took a quite different view of the scope for savings. In another authority it was clear that the 1991 rent increase was determined by the chair of finance and his ability to persuade the majority of the ruling party group, despite opposition from the director of housing, the chair of housing and others.

The purpose of this section has been to set out in general terms the process of producing local authority HRA budgets, and to convey some sense of the politics of the process and how authorities vary in their approach to decision making. What comes out of the case study work is that in all the authorities in the research, finance staff were central to the budgeting and financial arrangement process but that the degree of involvement of housing staff was much more variable. The influence of elected members also varied, but it was clear in several of the authorities studied that members played an important role in determining key rent and spending decisions. Officers perceived certain leading councillors - usually the chair of housing and the leader - as potentially very influential and powerful in the budget-making process.

The impact of the new financial regime

Given that one of the government's stated objectives for the NFR was that it should produce a pattern of rents which was more related to capital values, it is appropriate to group authorities according to initial rent levels and values. Thus the four categories are:

(i)   low rents, high values: Exeter, St Edmundsbury, Barking and Dagenham, and Hackney;

(ii) high rents, high values: Hammersmith and Fulham;

(iii) low rents, low values: North Tyneside;

(iv) high rents, low values: Middlesbrough.

Low rents, high values

The four authorities to be considered under this heading had all adopted low rent policies during the 1980s. Although their circumstances and politics were widely different there were some important similarities: Exeter, St Edmundsbury and Barking and Dagenham had all gone out of subsidy very early in the 1980s and were, therefore, free from direct government pressure on rents through the subsidy system. Another common factor was that these three authorities all had high levels of capital receipts, which, in different ways, helped to support the HRA. The situation in Hackney was rather different, for here the low rent policy of the 1980s was pursued despite the fact that the HRA continued to be subject to pressure on rents through the subsidy system.

In one sense this group of authorities with low rents and high values is the most interesting in terms of the impact of the NFR because it is the group in which the system seems designed to produce the greatest pressure on councils to raise rents. The evidence from the case studies is that the pressure on rents has indeed been quite considerable in Exeter, St Edmundsbury and Hackney, but much less severe in Barking and Dagenham.

Exeter entered the NFR from the position of having the lowest average rent in England and Wales in 1989/90, just £14.71 per week. The council had been hung since 1984, although Labour held all committee chairs and was in effective control, partly because of the cohesive and well-organised leadership within the Labour Group. In May 1991 Labour obtained control on the casting vote of committee chairs.

There was no general rent increase in Exeter in the three years before 1990, an achievement based on growing reserves of capital receipts which by 1989/90 yielded the equivalent of £7.00 per week for each tenancy. The guideline rent increase of £4.50 in 1990/91 thus represented an uplift of over 30%, compared to the overall national average increase of just 10%. In the first three years of the NFR Exeter's aggregate guideline increase amounted to £11.31 or 77%. At the same time the city has benefited from the targeting of M&M allowances in 1992/93, but the overall effect of the guideline and allowance system has been to raise notional rents by £8.61 per week more than the increase in allowances. In other words, less than a quarter of the notional rent increase is available to be spent on management and maintenance, and the rest is reflected in reduced subsidy.

How has the city council responded to this situation? In both 1990/91 and 1991/92 M&M expenditure exceeded allowances, but on the rent side the strategy has been to aim at increases in line with the guidelines. In the first year this was achieved mainly by drawing £500,000 (the equivalent of £1.40 on the average weekly rent) from balances brought forward, and in the second year the tactic was to transfer certain expenditure items out of the HRA and into the general fund. This again amounted to £500,000 and included costs associated with homelessness, housing advice, grounds maintenance and liaison with housing associations on development projects. It was felt that the inflation assumption for 1991/92 was quite unrealistic and required authorities to make cuts or other savings in order to hit the rent guideline, and in Exeter actual M&M expenditure was 5% below the previous year's level. In 1992/93 the effect of targeting reduced the pressure on the authority, although officers continued to perceive a demand from members for increased efficiency. However, the void rate in Exeter was only 0.63% in 1992, and rent arrears represented 1.8% of their total rent, implying a high level of performance by comparison with many other authorities.

St Edmundsbury is an authority based on the town of Bury St Edmunds and the surrounding, largely rural, area. Its housing stock of 7,856 in 1991/92 was somewhat larger than the stock in Exeter, and politically it is very different, having been controlled by the Conservatives since 1974. The average rent in 1989/90 was £16.38 which was one of the bottom 20 rents in the country. The NFR has assumed notional rent increases amounting to £10.45, or 64%, over three years. Over the same period the M&M allowance rose by only £110 per year, implying that only a fifth of the notional rent increase was available for spending on management and maintenance.

St Edmundsbury is one of a small number of authorities which have moved into negative subsidy which means that their entitlement to the housing element of HRA subsidy is a larger negative amount than their expenditure on rent rebates; in this situation they are required to make specific, non-discretionary transfers to their general funds. In 1990/91, 19 English authorities were in this position, and in 1991/92 the number was 14 (parliamentary answer dated 19.11.91). However, most of these authorities had transferred their housing stocks to new landlords and only two or three landlord authorities were in negative subsidy. In St Edmundsbury total net subsidy in 1990/91 was just £71,463, although expenditure on rent rebates was £3 million, implying a negative housing element of over £2.9 million. In 1991/92 expenditure on rebates rose to £3.1 million, but total net subsidy was minus £319,000, meaning that the authority had to transfer this amount to the general fund. HRA estimates for 1992/93 showed a negative subsidy of £650,000.

Before considering St Edmundsbury's response to the effect of the NFR, it is appropriate to look at how it came to be one of the first to lose all subsidy. There are two main factors. First, along with a number of other authorities, St Edmundsbury has been penalised since 1990/91 for 'overspending' in the late 1980s. The council had used its capital receipts to fund new building as it was entitled to do under the rules then in operation. The unit costs exceeded the approved cost limits, but the authority's view was that this was due to the limits being based on out of date figures rather than extravagant expenditure. However, when the NFR came into effect St Edmundsbury was penalised for this 'overspending'; the authority was deemed to have incurred inadmissible debt charges (even though the projects were funded from capital receipts rather than borrowing) and these inadmissible debt charges were then deducted from the opening credit ceiling. In other words, the authority was deemed to have a lower level of debt charges and was therefore entitled to a lower level of subsidy.

Nevertheless, this penalty might not have been enough on its own to exhaust subsidy entitlement. St Edmundsbury had behaved differently from many other authorities in the 1980s to the extent that it had used capital receipts to pay off debt, whereas others had invested or used up their receipts. In addition to the particular use to which receipts were put, there was the effect of the scale of receipts in the 1980s. Right to buy sales were buoyant, but in addition St Edmundsbury had extensive reserves of council owned land which it disposed of at high prices in 1986/87. It was, therefore, an authority with a high level of reserves compared to outstanding debt, and this was the major factor in eliminating HRA subsidy.

The council's response to the situation has been based on opposition to the principle of tenants having to contribute to, and in this case pay the whole of, rent rebate expenditure. Nevertheless, in the first two years of the NFR rent increases were above the guidelines; in 1990/91 the increase was £4.00, 55p above the guideline, and in 1991/92 the increase was £3.00, 50p above the guideline, but in 1992/93 members wanted to keep the increase below £4.00, and a figure of £3.98 was agreed against a guideline of £4.50. St Edmundsbury is an authority which has M&M spending levels well above allowances, hence the need to raise rents by more than guidelines. In 1992/93 the authority planned to make a revenue contribution to capital outlay of £440,000 to be funded by a 40% reduction in balances. This reflects the fact that St Edmundsbury received no borrowing approval in 1990/91 or 1991/92.

The third authority in this group is Hackney, an inner London borough with severe housing problems and a reputation as the poorest borough in the country. The council has been controlled by Labour for many years, and from 1982 to 1990 the Labour Group was dominated by leftist ideas, although in the 1990s a more moderate and pragmatic leadership is in place. During the 1980s Hackney consciously pursued a low rent policy with no rent increases between 1983 and 1987. As an alternative to raising rents, the council drew heavily on the general rate fund to a much greater extent than was assumed for rate support grant purposes; in 1988/89 the RFC was £27.4 million and in 1989/90 it was £29.5 million.

The NFR has had a significant impact in Hackney, much more significant, in fact, than would be inferred from the figures for guidelines and allowances. The guideline increases in the first three years were £4.50, £2.50 and £4.41, giving a total notional increase of £11.41. The increase in M&M allowances amounts to only £5.98 per week, although the authority did benefit from targeting of allowances in both 1991/92 and 1992/93.

The aggregate guideline rent increase in Hackney in the first three years of the NFR represented 56.6%, but the actual increase in this period was 101.4%. In April 1990 the rent increase was £5.33, compared with a guideline of £4.50, and the following year the increase was £6.33, against a guideline of just £2.50. This increase was also implemented two weeks early in order to generate more income, but the 1992 increase was both the largest ever in the borough, at £8.89, and introduced ten weeks early, in order to tackle the continuing HRA deficit.

One important factor is the difficulty that the borough has faced in controlling repair and maintenance spending. In the autumn of 1990 it was discovered that there was a large deficit, amounting to about £8 million on the account for 1989/90 due to overspending on maintenance. This raised the prospect of a large mid-year rent increase or cuts in services, since the option of a contribution from the general fund was closed off by the ring-fence around the HRA. However, decisions were not forthcoming in time for the problem to be resolved during that financial year and a deficit was carried forward into 1991/92. As early as June 1991 planning meetings were taking place with the intention of dealing with the problem and measures were put in place to contain the level of maintenance spending. Nevertheless, despite the 28% rent increase in January 1992 the HRA opened with another deficit in 1992/93.

Other important factors in Hackney have been the high levels of voids and rent arrears. The subsidy system operates on stringent assumptions about both these variables, and penalises authorities which exceed the allowances. The subsidy system assumes 2% voids, but in Hackney the void rate in early 1991 was 9.5%. In the case of arrears, authorities are assumed to collect 100% of rent due, and any arrears have to be accounted for in the year after they arise. Authorities are required to 'make provision' for bad and doubtful debts, which means that they have to build an appropriate amount into their HRA budgets. If, in practice, rent collection rates do not meet target levels then authorities have to increase provision for bad debts with consequential effects on rents. In Hackney the target was a collection rate of 95%, which was not achieved in 1990/91 and which, therefore, contributed to the rent increase in 1991/92.

The NFR has clearly had a major impact on rents in Hackney, and rents have risen far more than would have been the case if the previous system had continued. It can be said that the new system has created powerful new incentives for the authority to improve its housing management performance, and it is appropriate to add that there are two aspects of the NFR which are perceived to be beneficial to the borough. For authorities like Hackney, with a large proportion of local rate payers also being council tenants, the use of RFCs was not necessarily the best way to compensate for insensitivity in the subsidy system. The NFR has had the effect of relieving the local tax payers of the borough of a considerable financial burden. The ring-fencing of the HRA is also perceived by the director of housing to be beneficial to the housing service because it changes the culture of the organisation. The ring-fence gives the housing department a greater control of its costs, and can help to insulate it from cuts elsewhere in the authority.

Finally in this section we come to Barking and Dagenham, which, unlike the other authorities in this low rent, high value group, is remarkable for the relatively limited pressure exerted on rents by the working of the NFR since April 1990. Barking and Dagenham is a Labour-controlled authority in east London, and its 26,300 dwellings constitute about half the total supply of housing in the borough. It has long been unusual, especially in the London context, since it had the lowest rents in the capital (£16.16 in 1989/90) and the highest HRA surpluses for any Labour authority in the country. The explanation for this situation lies partly in the Labour Group's commitment to low rents, but the ability to maintain low rents alongside large HRA surpluses was mainly due to the age structure of the housing stock: just over half of the council stock was built between 1919 and 1939 which means that for many years Barking and Dagenham had exceptionally low debt charges. In addition, right to buy sales have been buoyant and the borough accumulated a huge reserve of capital receipts (£118 million in April 1989). A third key factor has been the cautious approach of the Labour Group, which, during the 1980s, preferred to use interest on accumulated capital receipts to keep rents low rather than to support a large capital programme.

Barking and Dagenham is the only one of the case study authorities to have been given the maximum guideline rent increase in each year of the NFR so far. The notional increase represents 71% of the 1989 average rent, but the amount of leverage exerted on the council to follow the guidelines has been mitigated by the relatively generous increase in M&M allowances, with the result that most (over 70%) of the rent increase has been available for spending. At the same time it is important to remember that Barking and Dagenham has received no HRA subsidy at all since the start of the NFR, and in 1990/91 and 1991/92 the borough was required to transfer £7.3 million and £4.5 million to the general fund. Like St Edmundsbury, Barking and Dagenham found itself in this negative subsidy situation because of the relationship between its capital reserves and its outstanding debts.

Unlike St Edmundsbury, however, Barking and Dagenham received a considerable windfall benefit in 1992/93 as a result of a surprise decision by the DOE in December 1991. It was decided that authorities which had both a negative entitlement to HRA subsidy and an M&M allowance below their target level should be given an allowance which was at the target level or as near to it as possible without the authority moving back into subsidy. In the case of Barking and Dagenham this meant both a 37% increase in M&M allowance and the elimination of the projected £4.5 million transfer to the general fund in 1992/93. Both of these outcomes were difficult to accommodate at that stage in the preparation of budgets.

Considering the borough's response to the NFR as a whole, it is clear that the council has been able to maintain a low rent policy since 1990. Actual rents have risen by only 57%. This is because of factors such as the relatively low level of M&M spending. Unlike a number of other case study authorities (Cardiff, Derwentside and Sandwell) Barking and Dagenham had not embarked on ambitious decentralisation programmes in 1989/90, thereby raising management expenditure too late to influence the calculation of the base level M&M allowance. Unlike a great many authorities, Barking and Dagenham actually underspent on management and maintenance in 1990/91 by comparison with its allowance, and in 1992/93 the huge increase in M&M allowance meant that there was no central government pressure on rents. However, the elimination of negative subsidy meant reduced income to the general fund. The timing of the DOE announcement meant that the council initially decided not to use the subsidy windfall to enhance repairs spending in 1992/93, but to use the money as a revenue contribution to the housing capital programme thereby preserving for other services capital reserves which had been scheduled for the housing programme. In this way the authority was able to cushion the loss to the general fund. Subsequently the council took a different approach and successfully sought a special determination of subsidy for 1992/93 to disapply the concession that authorities in surplus would have their M&M allowance calculated on the basis of the full target score.

High rents, high values

The case study authority which illustrates the group with high values and high rents is Hammersmith and Fulham, a Labour controlled inner London borough with the highest right to buy valuations in the country, apart from the neighbouring borough of Kensington and Chelsea. It also had the third highest average rent in 1989/90, £33.32 per week. The Labour Party has been in control since 1986, following a period of hung council in which the Conservatives were the largest party. The housing stock (18,500 dwellings in 1991/92 including 1,300 private sector leased dwellings) contains over 80% flats, reflecting the borough's inner-city location. These factors tend to produce high costs and Hammersmith and Fulham has a record as a high rent authority, although the current Labour leadership has a clear preference for low rent increases and a wish to move down the top ten.

The guideline increases in Hammersmith and Fulham have been £1.70, £2.50 and £4.05, amounting to £8.25, or 25% of the 1989/90 average rent. Thus in 1990/91 and 1992/93 the damping of guideline increases clearly mitigated the impact that the very high property valuations would otherwise have had. The M&M allowances are among the highest in the country, starting at £1,275 in 1990/91 and rising to £1,488 in 1992/93. The authority benefited from targeting in both 1991/92 and 1992/93.

Nevertheless, despite the benefits of targeting, the response to the NFR has been to raise rents by £11.88 over three years. In both 1990/91 and 1991/92 the actual rent increase was more than twice the guideline increase, but in 1992/93 political pressure resulted in an increase of £1.95 against a guideline of £4.05. The question, then, is why did the borough make such relatively large increases in the first two years? The first point to make is that the 1990/91 increase would have been even larger had it not been for two important mitigating factors. One was the decision to carry out a detailed review of the allocation of costs to different accounts; this resulted in expenditure of £4.9 million being switched from the HRA to the general fund (the equivalent of £5 off rents, but 85p on the poll tax). The other was, in effect, one final rate fund contribution of £2.8 million. As an authority with a history of RFCs, Hammersmith and Fulham did not normally have a working balance to carry forward, but at the transition from the old to the new system authorities were allowed to carry forward £150 per dwelling. Hammersmith and Fulham took advantage of the opportunity and budgeted to use this sum during 1990/91, leading to the conclusion that this represented a deferred rent increase with implications for 1991/92. There is a general point to be brought out here: money from such sources can only be spent once, but rent increases produce recurrent income.

Putting aside the issue of the deferred rent increase, the actual increase in 1990/91 was needed partly to meet expenditure in excess of allowances. In 1990/91 M&M spending was £118 per dwelling above the allowance, partly as a result of the low level of the M&M allowance in relation to established spending. Hammersmith and Fulham was one of the authorities which had capitalised repairs during the 1980s and, therefore, suffered a depression in its baseline M&M allowance. Targeting in subsequent years has gone some way towards making up the initial shortfall, but in 1991/92 M&M expenditure was again substantially above the allowance figure.

The rent increase of £5.95 in 1991/92 reflected the high M&M spending, the effect of the £3.35 deferred increase, and a significant amount, £2.39, which was due to subsidy changes affecting private sector leasing. There was, therefore, considerably more pressure on rents than might be inferred from a simple comparison of the rent guideline and the M&M allowance, and keeping the rent increase down to £5.95 required a considerable amount of effort by officers.

The use of private sector leasing as a way of providing for homeless people had grown rapidly in the late 1980s and was financially very attractive to hard-pressed inner London authorities like Hammersmith and Fulham. However, its attractiveness to the local authorities made it unattractive to central government which moved to change the subsidy regime in the autumn of 1990. The result is a transitional period of high costs falling on the HRA. Private sector leasing also has disadvantages for the authority in that it is more difficult to manage and has significantly higher levels of voids and rent arrears than the council's own stock, thereby adding to the costs to be borne by the HRA.

In 1992/93 there was a political requirement, clearly set out by the leadership, that the rent increase should be below the guideline level if at all possible. In order to achieve such an increase real savings were required and here the recession and the renewal of the Direct Services Organisation (DSO) contract provided the necessary relief. The DSO, in competition with private sector contractors, put in lower tender prices for housing maintenance, thereby helping to produce an acceptable rent increase.

Low rents, low values

Amongst the case study authorities the one which falls into this category is North Tyneside, with an average rent level of £16.31 at April 1989. A metropolitan district consisting of Wallsend, North Shields, Tynemouth, Whitley Bay and other smaller settlements, North Tyneside has been Labour controlled since its creation in 1974. During the 1980s the Labour Group was more left-wing than it is now, and contained an element which was determined to keep rents and rent increases to a minimum using RFCs and/or capitalisation of repairs to maintain standards of service. There was only one general rent increase in the six years up to September 1989. However, there was a £3.00 increase half way through 1989/90.

Like Hammersmith and Fulham, North Tyneside made use of capitalised repairs during the 1980s, but to a much greater extent. During the three crucial years 1986/87 to 1988/89 North Tyneside had recorded revenue-funded repairs averaging just £545,000 per annum, while capitalised repairs expenditure averaged £6.9 million. On this basis, therefore, North Tyneside was awarded the lowest M&M allowance at the start of the NFR. As discussed in Chapter 3, North Tyneside, supported by the AMA, contested the very low M&M allowance on the grounds that it did not fairly reflect what was actually being spent on the stock. The result was that the allowance was raised from £293 to £508, which was regarded by officers in North Tyneside as a figure they could live with. In subsequent years the allowance has benefited from targeting.

As an authority with low property values, North Tyneside has been given the minimum guideline rent increase each year. The aggregate notional rent increase of £3.53 represents only 18% of the average rent after the September 1989 increase, and taking into account the effects of targeting it seems that North Tyneside has not been under serious pressure to raise rents. The leverage on rents implied by the gap between the increases in guideline and allowance is very small at £21.00 per annum, compared with figures of over £8.00 per week quoted earlier for Exeter and Bury St Edmunds.

In practice, North Tyneside has been able to continue its low rent policy, although, because of the mid-year increase in 1989 the average actual rent remains about 50p above the notional average. Following the £3.00 per week increase in September 1989, the council made no increase at all in April 1990 at a time when rents generally were rising by about 15%. In both 1991/92 and 1992/93 the council was able to budget for rent increases below guideline levels, although it appeared that keeping increases below inflation was the main objective.

High rents, low values

In 1989/90 Middlesbrough had the third highest rents outside London (behind Spelthorne and Torbay) but as a Labour controlled industrial town in the North East it was a most unlikely place to find such high rents. In 1989/90 its average rent of £27.75 was £7.95 above the regional average, and more in line with rents in inner London. The explanation for high rents in Middlesbrough is that during the 1970s and 1980s Middlesbrough maintained a high level of capital investment, resulting in correspondingly high debt charges. Expenditure on debt charges in Middlesbrough was significantly higher than in other authorities with comparable rents. The authority was also handicapped by low right to buy valuations in the 1980s, leading to low levels of usable capital receipts. In addition, the leaders of the Labour Group, and in particular the chair of housing, were committed to a policy of providing for a local population amongst whom there was a high level of need for rented housing (81% of council tenants receive housing benefit).

In addition to the impact of high capital charges, Middlesbrough's high rents reflected a relatively high level of M&M spending, at least by comparison with other authorities in the northern region (in 1990/91 it was the only authority in the region to have an M&M allowance above £700).

The NFR has imposed little direct leverage on rents, although more than in some other northern authorities which have benefited from targeting on M&M allowances. Middlesbrough has had the minimum guideline rent increase each year since the start of the NFR, and standard percentage increases in M&M allowances. As a high rent authority with low property values, Middlesbrough benefited from low percentage guideline rent increases; the guideline increase of 95p in 1990/91 (just 3.4%) clearly represented a lesser political problem for local councillors than some of the very high percentage increases referred to earlier in the low rent, high value areas (eg in Exeter and St Edmundsbury). Middlesbrough's combination of high rents and low values meant that without damping in 1990/91 it would have had an implied rent reduction of £15.87 per week - the largest reduction in the country.

In practice the council agreed to a rent increase in line with the guideline in 1990/91, although M&M spending fell significantly below the allowance by £95.00 per dwelling per year. In the following year the rent increase was £1.20, or 18p below the guideline, but in 1992/93 the increase was £2.50, more than twice the guideline. Thus the effect of this large increase is that after three years Middlesbrough has rents at £1.12 above the guideline, but this is a relatively small amount compared with many other authorities. What is significant here is that Middlesbrough underspent against its M&M allowances in both 1990/91 and 1991/92.

Middlesbrough is interesting as an authority which had been committed to a large capital programme and which perceives itself as having been badly affected by the new capital controls. As a response, the authority has allocated large sums of HRA expenditure to RCCOs in each year of the NFR, although it had not previously done so. In 1990/91, £438,405 was spent supporting the capital programme, and in 1991/92 the amount rose to £2 million. Almost all of the RCCO in 1991/92 was funded from HRA balances, which fell from over £3.1 million at the start of 1991/92 to just under £1 million in 1992/93.

Discussion

Before leaving the case studies, it is appropriate to make some reference to the authorities which have not been discussed above and to draw out some general comments. Two authorities, Sandwell and Knowsley, had re-opened their accounts for earlier years in order to de-capitalise repairs in the three years which were crucial for the calculation of baseline M&M allowances. Knowsley had achieved an allowance significantly above its M&M target spending level and officers expressed concern about the possibility of the allowance being cut back to the target level: this would have a greater impact because actual spending was running well above allowance. In Cardiff M&M spending had risen substantially during a period of decentralisation and service growth in the late 1980s, and actual expenditure in 1991/92 was 12% over allowance.

Torbay was involved in one of the first attempted large-scale voluntary transfers, in 1988, and officers felt that decisions made at that time were continuing adversely to affect the authority. At the time of the attempted transfer the council had cut back on capital expenditure and had not increased M&M expenditure, but after the collapse of the transfer both categories of spending had increased sharply, although too late to be reflected in capital allocations and the baseline M&M allowance after 1990/91. Thus, the authority perceived itself to be suffering under the NFR because of decisions which at the time were seen to be in the spirit of government policy.

Another point from Torbay was the suggestion that the capital side of the NFR was more significant than the revenue side; this point has already emerged from the Middlesbrough case study and it was a perspective shared by officials in Leicester. On the morning in February 1991 that the researcher arrived to start the case study work, senior officers in the city were pre-occupied by receipt of a letter from the DOE in London reversing a verbal assurance (by the DOE regional office) that a supplementary credit approval of £1.9 million for 1990/91 would be forthcoming to cover increased expenditure on improvement grants. This was a very serious development for an authority at that point in the financial year, and it was especially important for an authority which placed great emphasis on its leading role in private sector renewal. The more general point to be brought out here is that the NFR makes it more difficult for authorities to meet priorities in the private sector, not just because of the cutback in resources but also because of the reduced flexibility in the use of capital funds.

Turning now to the case study authorities as a group, it is important to record that two-thirds of them have diverged from the guidelines and allowances. Five have aggregate rent increases of more than twice the guideline increases, and a further four have increases of at least 40% above guideline over the first three years of the system. Only Barking and Dagenham has diverged significantly from the guideline rent by making low rent increases. Some of the reasons for divergence have been discussed above, but it is appropriate to add a reference to some of the other authorities.

Sandwell, Derwentside and Rhymney Valley, for example, had all incurred higher management costs as a result of decentralisation or restructuring designed to improve the quality of service offered to tenants, but they had done so after the base years for the calculation of M&M allowances.

Cotswold and Derwentside have both opted for large RCCOs, which were inevitably reflected in higher rents. Altogether seven of the case study authorities have resorted to RCCOs since the start of the NFR, in order to support expenditure on their housing stock in a period of reduced capital resources.

Another point to mention here is that some of the case study authorities have drawn heavily on working balances to support HRA expenditure, but the pattern is not consistent. Some authorities which ran down their balances in 1990/91 built them up again in 1991/92, while others did the opposite. In all the authorities where balances were discussed, the importance of keeping a reasonable working balance was well understood, especially in the new environment in which there is no possibility of movement of funds between the HRA and the general fund.

Overall, the case studies illustrate the variety of circumstances, priorities and responses across the country in the first three years of the NFR. They show very clearly how difficult it is for central government to achieve its desired outcomes and to permit authorities the freedom to respond to local problems in their own ways.

CONCLUSIONS

The NFR is very much a product of its time. First, in the sense that it requires the production and analysis of large amounts of technical data to a degree that would have been difficult to contemplate before the introduction of modern information technology when there were 1,400 housing authorities rather than the 400 of today. Second, it is designed to respond to the contemporary problem of HRA surpluses in an era of declining stock levels. And third, it is based on policy objectives dominated by concerns about pricing and the control of public expenditure. It is about steering authorities towards rents which are more closely linked to property values in the private market, and about continuing the trend towards greater reliance on means-tested assistance rather than general housing subsidy.

It is, however, a system which shows considerable continuity with the past in the retention of policy mechanisms such as the notional HRA and in the continuation of trends such as the shift from general to means-tested subsidy and the erosion of local authority freedom and flexibility. The NFR is to be understood as a development from the 1980 Act system to the extent that it is a more sophisticated approach to technical problems of subsidy distribution, and a more hard-nosed approach to central-local relations. After the 1980 system was undermined by local authority opposition and evasion, the NFR represents a good example of the top trying to "get a better grip on the situation" (Ham and Hill, 1984, p 110).

As explained in Chapter 2, the government was concerned to achieve a number of objectives. It was driven by a desire to gain control of subsidy expenditure and to establish a closer relationship between what tenants paid in rent and the service that they received. Ministers were particularly concerned about three groups of authorities: those that kept rents low and allowed the housing stock to deteriorate; those that kept rents low and used RFCs to maintain services, and those that pushed rents up and used HRA surpluses to subsidise the general rates fund. The NFR has been very effective in reducing local authority flexibility. Before 1990 authorities wishing to operate low rent policies could do so by adopting a variety of tactics: low spending, RFCs, using interest on capital receipts, capitalisation of repairs or improved efficiency. Now only the first and last of these options are available.

Local authorities can still opt for a policy of low rents and low expenditure, although the evidence suggests that few have adopted this route (among the case study authorities only Barking and Dagenham and, arguably, North Tyneside fall into this category). Low rents and high expenditure were only possible where authorities could draw on RFCs or interest from capital receipts, and since these sources of HRA income have been closed off in the NFR, this strategy is no longer available (and case study authorities such as Hackney and Exeter have been forced to change). High rents and low expenditure were only attractive to authorities wishing to use the HRA as a source of income for the general rate fund or to give tenants an incentive to vote for voluntary transfer (as in the case of Torbay in 1988). Now, however, only the latter continues as a reason and none of the case study authorities has pursued voluntary transfer since 1990.

The option of high rents and high expenditure remains a possibility, and one of the main findings of this and other research (Association of District Councils, 1990; 1991; Association of Metropolitan Authorities, 1990; 1991; Association of Metropolitan Authorities/Association of District Councils, 1992) is that most authorities have opted to raise rents above guideline levels in order to support expenditure above allowances, although to very different degrees and for diverse reasons. Hackney, for instance, illustrates a category of authority which has been forced to make large rent increases as it has struggled to bring costs under control and to improve its performance on voids and arrears. Cotswold represents a different category; here the council had very high levels of M&M spending in the late 1980s as capital expenditure was funded from revenue producing an initial M&M allowance well above target, and therefore the allowances here have been cut in real terms in 1991/92 and 1992/93. Cotswold's high rents and expenditure may be seen as acts of defiance by an authority seeking to defend a locally determined level of service against a centrally imposed alternative view of what is appropriate. The statistical evidence indicates that on average Conservative councils tended to increase rents and expenditure more than other councils, after allowing for other factors.

There is some evidence to suggest that M&M spending generally was rising in the late 1980s, although too late to be fully reflected in the baseline calculation of M&M allowances, and it is quite clear that authorities have continued the upward trend, despite the pressures within the NFR. It is important to recognise that the government's criticism of local authorities for low M&M spending has not fed through to M&M allowances which encourage significantly higher levels of spending. Some authorities have experienced two years in which their allowances have risen by less than the assumed rate of inflation. However, some other authorities that have benefited from targeting are, in effect, being compensated for the government's refusal in 1989 to take capitalised repairs expenditure into account in the calculation of initial M&M allowances.

As a system which relies on leverage, the NFR can apply pressure on authorities only by withdrawing or increasing subsidy. Because authorities are generally reluctant to reduce spending on management and maintenance, withdrawal of subsidy is very good at making them raise rents. In areas where the government wishes to increase both rents and M&M spending, the increases in guideline rents and M&M allowances will tend to cancel one another out, leaving the authorities free to make their own decisions. The point here is that the government has stated objectives about the need to raise rents and to encourage higher levels of M&M spending in certain areas, but it has only one policy instrument, the giving or withholding of subsidy, by which to pursue these objectives. This invites the conclusion that the prime concern is with rents. It also prompts the observation that an inefficient authority is unlikely to be made more efficient by a reduction in subsidy - it is probably too crude a device for a task as complex as improving the efficiency and effectiveness of a housing authority. How much authorities respond to the general incentives in the new regime depends in part on the political sensitivity of rents. Both prior reasoning and the statistical evidence support the view that local authorities are less likely to cut spending than to raise rents when subsidy is withdrawn, and to increase spending rather than cut rents when subsidy is increased.

The outcomes in terms of rent increases across the country since 1990/91 indicate the success of the NFR in delivering both substantial real increases in average rent levels, and a widening of rent differentials between high and low cost areas. The regional pattern of rents in 1992 is quite close to the pattern of market values, but this does reflect the exceptionally depressed state of the housing market in the south of England at this time.

Both rents and M&M expenditure have increased more than government guidelines. Essentially, simultaneous increases in M&M spending are despite rather than because of the system. Indeed, as authorities have raised rents by more than guidelines in order to finance higher M&M expenditure, they have unwittingly set up a situation in which it is more likely that in future years rents will again have to exceed guidelines if service levels are to be maintained. When rents exceed guidelines there is a tendency for the level of rent rebate subsidy to rise, and reference has been made in Chapter 3 to the substantial overruns on rebate subsidy in the first two years of the NFR. The response from the Treasury to this kind of budgetary problem is to press for the overrun to be recouped in the following year, by insisting on a bigger gap between guidelines and allowances, so as to put more pressure on rents and to reduce subsidy.

It has been argued above that the NFR works by the application of leverage on rents; the severity of the leverage being dependent upon the year-on-year change in the relationship between the guideline rent increase and the M&M allowance. But leverage is a device which carries a price for the centre. A high degree of leverage can be produced only at the price of politically risky high guideline rent increases, or very low M&M allowances. The evidence suggests that while ministers want to see rents rising they are concerned not to be seen as responsible for very high increases, and this tends to produce a bias towards low M&M settlements.

This may lead to a situation in which M&M allowances are seen to be held down for public expenditure and financial management reasons, and this may further undermine the credibility of the allowances as indicators of what needs to be spent on the stock. If this were to happen then it would also undermine the standing of guideline rents as credible indicators of what should be charged in order to provide a satisfactory standard of service.

The finding that total repairs and maintenance spending has fallen by 23% overall, and as much as 57% in London, due to the impact of the new capital control system alongside the new revenue regime, rather reinforces the point just made. While management expenditure is on a strongly rising trend in real terms, expenditure on the stock has suffered a sharp reduction. This is in spite of the well-known and large backlog of repair work in the council stock. Inadequate resources for management and maintenance would be somewhat more bearable if it were felt that these resources were well targeted. In fact, progress with targeting within the NFR has been slow, and the statistical evidence presented in Chapter 4 showed that the spending outcomes do not represent any improvement in targeting. Repairs and maintenance expenditure is less well targeted than it was in 1987/88. One factor underlying this situation is the fact that authorities that had more favourable financial conditions under the pre 1990 regime have been able to carry some of the benefit of this through into the new regime.

This suggests that the NFR is not yet achieving equity between areas and authorities. Part of the reason is that some of the factors affecting HRA costs and incomes were not fully covered by subsidy adjustments in the transition to the NFR. These factors tend to affect London disproportionately. While moves toward greater equity would be feasible and desirable, it is unlikely that a completely idealised system can be evolved to cater for all local circumstances. The extent to which particular local circumstances lead to divergences between guidelines and actual rents or expenditures is very striking, from both the statistical and the case study evidence. In part, these divergences represent local factors outside the immediate control of authorities, and in part they represent the continued exercise of local discretion.

What, then, of the future of the NFR? Is it more robust than its predecessor, which, although it survived for a decade, was fatally wounded as early as 1981 when the secretary of state agreed not to insist that authorities transferred HRA surpluses to their general rates funds? From the government's point of view the NFR has been successful in pushing up rents and in reducing the level of subsidy. The government has secured control of the housing element of HRA subsidy, although falling levels of council house sales tend to hold back the rate at which this element of subsidy falls. The government has also eliminated locally funded subsidy, but it has not obtained control of the rent rebate element of the subsidy and this is clearly problematic.

The NFR may be seen as a success in policy terms, but in financial terms it is less successful. The DOE is under pressure from the Treasury to keep within its budget and when budgets are exceeded then action is required. When the subsidy bill rose rapidly in 1990/91 because of the effects of private sector leasing, the Treasury insisted that the rules be changed. It seems inevitable, therefore, that the Treasury will seek to cap rent rebate expenditure. If authorities increase the use of RCCOs, as advocated by the Audit Commission (1992), then this would be likely to hasten action on rebates because large-scale rent increases to fund RCCOs would have a knock-on effect on rebate expenditure.

How much further can rents be pushed up? Housing benefit represents one type of limit, as explained above. Implicit in any move to 'cap' housing benefit because authorities are increasing their rents above guidelines is an assumption that local decision makers are less sensitive to rent increases than they might have been in the past, due to the effect of high housing benefit dependence. The evidence from this study suggests that such tendencies may be present, but this evidence is not very conclusive. There may also be limits to rents on grounds of affordability, including limiting the poverty trap effect of rebates as well as the problems of low income households not eligible for housing benefit. Market values or rents must ultimately place some upper limit on local authority rents. Rents are already reaching the point of matching the regional variation in market values, albeit in a depression. What the 'right' ratio of rent to market value should be has never been stated by the government, so we do not know at what point the average level of rents would reach market levels. However, at the time of writing, housing associations in the south of England are beginning to worry that their rents may be exceeding market rents.

As far as the local authorities are concerned the NFR has brought some real advantages. The ring-fencing of the HRA is perceived to have brought benefits in terms of clarifying the costs which properly fall on the account, and the banning of RFCs is seen as beneficial in circumstances where most ratepayers were also tenants. However, the NFR has undeniably reduced the flexibility of local authority responses to local housing problems, and there is much criticism of the amalgamation of general housing subsidy and rent rebate subsidy in a way which appears to make better off tenants pay the rebates of their poorer neighbours.

Although the present government is unlikely to uncouple the two parts of the HRA subsidy, the NFR has not yet settled down to a steady state and is unlikely to do so. It is probable that it will continue to evolve and change. The detailed specification of the ring-fence is one area where further action can be expected, and reference has already been made to the probability of action affecting rent rebate subsidy. If authorities faced capping of their rent rebate subsidy then this could increase the rate at which authorities went out of subsidy altogether, and could lead to demands for change. The complexity of the system is another issue which might lead to pressure from within the DOE for changes of a simplifying nature, and simplification might lead to a pattern of incentives and outcomes which would generate demands for further change. There are, then, reasons to expect continuing changes to the financial regime but at this stage it seems likely that these will be in the form of amendments to the system, within the framework of the existing legislation, although the history of housing subsidies in Britain suggests that further legislation cannot be too far in the future.

GLOSSARY

Annual capital guideline (ACG) - the initial allocation of capital spending permission determined for each local authority by central government each year, based on needs formulae and judgements about the authority's Housing Investment Programme (see below).

Assumed national rent - average of guideline rents (see below).

Basic credit approval (BCA) - the amount of borrowing for general capital expenditure purposes which local authorities are allowed to incur as determined by central government each year. Additional capital spending may be financed from part of capital receipts, from supplementary credit approvals (see below) or from revenue. BCA is based on annual capital guideline, less receipts taken into account (see below), plus specified grants (see below).

Capital expenditure - expenditure on the acquisition of assets such as land and buildings which provide a use or benefit over several years. Major repairs or renewals which add to the life or value of buildings may be counted as capital (known as 'capitalised repairs').

Capital receipts - sums of money received by local authorities from the sale of capital assets, particularly council houses sold under the right to buy.

Capitalised repairs - see capital expenditure (above).

Credit ceiling - the amount of outstanding debt relating to housing which is allowed for in the calculation of subsidy in the notional housing revenue account (see below). Each year the credit ceiling is adjusted to include new borrowing and to exclude repayments of debt.

Damping - a constraint upon the amount that both rent guidelines and maintenance and management allowances are allowed to change each year.

Deferred purchase - an unconventional method of financing capital projects employed by some local authorities in the 1980s to circumvent the capital expenditure control rules then in operation, which has the effect of putting off the costs of purchase into future years.

Direct Services Organisation (DSO) - separate part of local authority organisation which provides specified services, such as council house maintenance, under compulsory competitive tendering arrangements and subject to strict accounting rules and profit targets. Between 1981 and 1988 these arrangements applied in a more limited way to council house building and maintenance by what were then called Direct Labour Organisations.

Economic subsidy - subsidy (see below) assessed with reference to the current cost of housing based on today's values, rather than on the basis of historic cost accounting (see below).

General fund transfers - under the new financial regime since 1990, when a local authority receives no housing revenue account subsidy (see below) it must transfer an amount equal to the notional negative subsidy from its HRA to its general fund. Between 1981 and 1989, local authorities had the power to transfer surpluses from their HRA to their general rate fund.

General housing subsidy - see housing element of subsidy (below).

Generalised needs index (GNI) - a composite statistical index which measures the need for investment in housing by local authorities, compiled by the Department of the Environment for regions and local authority areas, and used as a partial basis for the allocation of annual capital guidelines (see above).

Grant related expenditure (GRE) - see standard spending assessment (below).

Historic cost accounting - method of accounting for capital assets in which the charge for capital is based upon the debt repayments and interest on outstanding debt, where debt depends upon the history of past capital investments and methods of financing and bears no relationship to present values. This method is normal local authority practice, included in housing revenue accounts.

Housing benefit - assistance with housing costs is provided to low income tenants in the form of a rent rebate, which may meet all the rent (eg for a tenant on income support) or a part of it. The rebate depends upon the level of the rent, the composition of the household, and the net income of the tenant. Since 1984 rebates have been known as housing benefit.

Housing element of subsidy - under the NFR since 1990, local authorities have received a combined subsidy for housing including the cost of rebates (housing revenue account subsidy, see below). The housing element is the subsidy for general housing costs, excluding the cost of the income-related rebates, and replaces the previous exchequer subsidies and rate fund contributions. The housing element can be and frequently is a negative amount.

Housing investment programme (HIP) - annual statement of local housing strategy, statistical information about housing conditions and needs, and proposed programme of capital expenditure, produced by each local authority and submitted to the Department of the Environment as a basis for discussion and subsequent allocation of capital resources (ACGs, SCGs, SCAs, as defined elsewhere).

Housing revenue account (HRA) - standard form of account maintained by all local housing authorities in which they record annual expenditure incurred and income received in respect of their role as landlords of rented housing (ie council housing).

Housing revenue account subsidy - the total subsidy paid by central government to a local authority's housing account (HRA), including a general amount and an amount for rent rebates (housing benefit). The subsidy equals the difference between expenditure including rebates and income from rents and other sources in the notional HRA (see below).

Leverage - a pressure or incentive on local authorities to behave in a particular way; for example, withdrawal of subsidy provides upwards leverage on rents.

Maintenance and management (M&M) allowance - the amount of expenditure (in pounds per dwelling per year) which the government assumes each local authority can spend on repair and maintenance and on supervision and management, in calculating entitlement to subsidy. The allowance is based on an M&M target (see below) and past spending.

Maintenance and management (M&M) target - an estimate of the amount of expenditure (in pounds per dwelling per year) which each local authority needs to spend to provide a reasonable standard of service in both maintenance and management, based on a formula taking account of characteristics of the housing stock and other factors.

New financial regime (NFR) - the new rules and arrangements for council housing accounting (HRAs), subsidies and capital expenditure and financing controls introduced in April 1990 on the basis of the 1989 Local Government and Housing Act.

Non-prescribed expenditure - in the 1980s local authorities were allowed to spend 'prescribed proportions' (between 20% and 50%) of capital receipts on new capital projects. However, they were also allowed to spend part or all of the remaining receipts on capitalised repairs to council housing, and this was referred to as 'non-prescribed expenditure'.

Notional housing revenue account - version of standard HRA (see above) which records income and expenditure under certain rules and assumptions prescribed by the Department of the Environment, the purpose of which is to calculate subsidy. For example, M&M expenditure is based on the allowance (see above) while rent income is based on the guideline (see below).

Public Expenditure Survey Committee (PESC) - interdepartmental official committee of central government, chaired by the Treasury, which manages the annual process of decision-making on public expenditure leading up to the production to the Autumn Statement and Departmental Annual Reports (formerly known as the Public Expenditure or PESC White Papers).

Rate fund contribution (RFC) - prior to 1990 local authorities were able to transfer money to their HRAs from their general accounts, financed from general grants and the local tax, which at that time was the rates (hence the name rate fund). In 1990 this power was removed by the so-called 'ring-fencing' of HRAs (see below), but existing contributions were absorbed in central subsidies. Between 1981 and 1989 it was possible to transfer money both ways between the rate fund and the HRA.

Receipts taken into account (RTIA) - the makes an annual allocation of permission to borrow and spend on capital projects to each local authority. This allocation is based on formulae and judgements about need, and is then adjusted to make partial allowance for the capital receipts that the authority is expected to have available to finance capital spending, based on previous years' amounts of actual receipts.

Rent guidelines - local authorities are notified each year of an amount (in pounds per dwelling per week) of the increase in rent which the government assumes that they can make, in calculating entitlement to subsidy. The authority can increase rents by more or less, but the subsidy is calculated on the assumption that the rent increase equals the guideline.

Rent rebates - see housing benefit (above).

Revenue contributions to capital outlay (RCCO) - most local authority capital expenditure (investment) is financed either by borrowing or by the use of capital receipts. However, capital expenditure may be paid for directly from the HRA, in which case it is known as RCCO and paid for directly by the tenants in the form of higher rents.

Revenue expenditure - local authorities incur expenditure either on capital items (see above) or on recurrent items like staffing and running costs. Recurrent expenditure, including the costs of repaying and servicing debts, are accounted for in what are called 'revenue accounts', of which the HRA is one.

Right to buy - following the 1980 Housing Act most council tenants have had the right to buy their council home, at a substantial discount on market value and if necessary with a 100% council mortgage. Approximately 1.5 million tenants, a quarter of the 1980 total, have taken advantage of this opportunity.

Ring-fencing - until 1989 local authorities were able to transfer money in or out of their HRAs (see rate fund contributions, general fund transfers), but the 1989 Local Government and Housing Act prevents such transfers except in limited circumstances. This provision is known as 'ring-fencing'; the term also refers to a recommended but not yet mandatory set of rules about exactly what kinds of expenditure (and income) may legitimately be charged to the HRA, with the intention of making it a strict 'landlord account' which does not include general social or community service costs.

Short term leasing - a method of acquiring the use of privately rented dwellings to provide temporary accommodation for the homeless. This was used increasingly in the late 1980s, especially in London, but changes in the new financial regime made it less financially viable for local authorities.

Specified capital grants (SCGs) - capital expenditure on certain housing activities which are not directly related to council housing, chiefly improvement grants to private owners, are eligible for a capital grant from the government, normally at a rate of 75%. These grants are called specified capital grants and each authority receives a separate allocation of an amount which the government will reimburse each year.

Standard spending assessment (SSA) - the amount each local authority is estimated to need to spend each year on its general fund to provide a standard level of service, as calculated by the government in order to distribute the revenue support grant and in part to determine expenditure limits. SSA refers to net revenue expenditure on the general range of local government services excluding council housing. Prior to 1990 the equivalent system was known as grant related expenditure (GRE) and did include an allowance for rate fund contributions to council housing.

Subsidy - the difference between what tenants pay and the cost of providing the housing.

Supplementary credit approvals (SCAs) - additional permissions to borrow to finance capital expenditure on approved, specific projects, for example Estate Action or City Challenge schemes.

Voids - dwellings which are vacant, and consequently producing no rental income.

Working Balance - amount of money in the HRA at beginning or end of financial year; local authorities are not allowed to budget for a deficit on the account but they may plan to increase or reduce their working balance.

REFERENCES

Audit Commission (1986a) *Managing the crisis in council housing*, London: HMSO.

Audit Commission (1986b) *Improving council house maintenance*, London: HMSO.

Audit Commission (1992) *Developing local authority housing strategies*, London: HMSO.

Association of District Councils (1990) *Survey on council house rents, housing subsidy and capital expenditure*, London: ADC.

Association of District Councils (1991) *Survey on council house rents, housing subsidy and capital expenditure 1991/92*, London: ADC.

Association of Metropolitan Authorities (1990) *Survey of the effects of the new financial regime for local authority housing*, London: AMA.

Association of Metropolitan Authorities (1991) *New financial regime survey report 1991/92*, London: AMA.

Association of Metropolitan Authorities /Association of District Councils (1992) *AMA/ADC housing finance survey report 1992/93*, London: AMA/ADC.

Barrett, S. and Fudge, C. (eds) (1981) *Policy and action*, London: Methuen.

Bramley, G (1991) *Bridging the affordability gap in 1990: an update of research on housing access and affordability*, Birmingham: BEC Publications.

Crook, T., Kemp, P., Anderson, I. and Bowman, S. (1991) *Tax incentives and the revival of private renting*, York: Cloister Press.

Department of the Environment (1988) *New financial regime for local authority housing in England and Wales: a consultation paper*, London: DOE.

Department of the Environment and Welsh Office (1977) *Housing policy: a consultative document*, Cmnd 6851, London: HMSO.

Department of the Environment and Welsh Office (1987) *Housing: the government's proposals*, Cm 214, London: HMSO.

Elmore, R. (1980) 'Backward mapping: implementation research and policy decisions', *Political Science Quarterly*, pp 601-16.

Forrest, R. and Murie, A. (1985) *An unreasonable act? Central-local government conflict and the Housing Act 1980*, Bristol: SAUS Publications, University of Bristol.

Forrest, R. and Murie, A. (1988) *Selling the welfare state*, London: Routledge.

Forrest, R. and Murie, A. (1992) 'The right to buy', in C. Grant (ed) *Built to last? Reflections on British housing policy*, London: Shelter.

Garnett, D., Reid, B. and Riley, H. (1991) *Housing finance*, Harlow: Longman, 2nd edition.

Gibb, K. and Munro, M. (1991) *Housing finance in the UK: an introduction*, Basingstoke: Macmillan.

Ham, C. and Hill, M. (1984) *The policy process in the modern capitalist state*, Oxford: Blackwell.

Hepworth, N. (1984) *The finance of local government*, London: Allen and Unwin, 7th edition.

Hills, J. (1991) *Unravelling housing finance*, Oxford: Clarendon Press.

Houlihan, B. (1988) *Housing and central-local government relations*, Aldershot: Gower.

Ingram, H. and Schneider, A. (1990) 'Improving implementation through framing smarter statutes', *Journal of Public Policy*, vol 10, no 1, pp 67-88.

Jackson, A. and Kleinman, M. (1992) *A normative study of local authority housing management costs*, London: HMSO.

Joseph Rowntree Foundation (1991) *Inquiry into British housing, second report*, York: Joseph Rowntree Foundation.

Karn, V. (1993) 'Remodelling a HAT: the implementation of the Housing Action Trust legislation 1987-92', in P. Malpass and R. Means (eds) *Implementing housing policy*, Milton Keynes: Open University Press.

Kemp, P. (1988) *The future of private renting*, Salford: University of Salford.

Kemp, P. (1993) 'Rebuilding the private rented sector?' in P. Malpass and R. Means (eds) *Implementing housing policy*, Milton Keynes: Open University Press.

Lansley, S. (1979) *Housing and public policy*, Beckenham: Croom Helm.

Maclennan, D., Gibb, K. and More, A. (1991) *Fairer subsidies, faster growth*, York: Joseph Rowntree Foundation.

Malpass, P. (1990) *Reshaping housing policy*, London: Routledge.

Malpass, P. (1992) 'Investment strategies', in C. Grant (ed) *Built to last? Reflections on British housing policy*, London: Shelter.

Malpass, P. (1993) 'Housing policy and the housing system since 1979', in P. Malpass and R. Means (eds) *Implementing housing policy*, Milton Keynes: Open University Press.

Malpass, P. and Murie, A. (1990) *Housing policy and practice*, Basingstoke: Macmillan, 3rd edition.

Merrett, S. (1979) *State housing in Britain*, London: Routledge and Kegan Paul.

National Federation of Housing Associations (1985) *Inquiry into British housing: the report*, London: National Federation of Housing Associations.

Power, A. (1987) *The crisis in council housing: is public housing manageable?* London: London School of Economics, Welfare State Project Discussion Paper 21.

Price Waterhouse (1992) *Empirical study into the costs of local authority housing management*, London: HMSO.

Platt, S. (1987) 'Yes Minister, but ...', *Roof*, January/February, pp 23-25.

Pressman, J. and Wildavsky, A. (1973) *Implementation*, Berkeley: University of California Press.

Randolph, B. (1993) 'The reprivatisation of housing associations', in P. Malpass and R. Means (eds) *Implementing housing policy*, Milton Keynes: Open University Press.

Rhodes, R. (1981) *Control and power in central-local government relations*, Farnborough: Gower.

Webber, R. and Craig, J. (1978) 'Socio-economic classification of local authority areas', *OPCS Studies on Medical and Population Subjects*, no 35, London: HMSO.

Woodward, R. (1991) 'Mobilising opposition: the campaign against housing action trusts in Tower Hamlets', *Housing Studies*, vol 6, no 1, pp 44-56.

Young, G. (1991) 'Our shared commitment', *Roof*, November/December, pp 8-9.